Road

Rage

Herculaneum, Missouri

Although the author and publisher have exhaustively researched all resources to ensure the accuracy and completeness of the information contained in this book, we assume no responsibility for errors, inaccuracies, omissions, or any other inconsistencies herein. Any slights against people or organizations are unintentional and similarities among persons coincidental. Many of the road rage and aggressive driving incidents described in this book occurred prior to trial of certain alleged offenders. Therefore, any or all of the alleged offenders may have been found innocent before or after publication of these sources. Therefore, this book makes no assertion of guilt toward any party or parties, but rather, only repeats what has already been reported and published in the news media, in police reports, and other sources. The author and publisher make no guarantees or recommendations with regard to any agency or organization listed anywhere in this book. Readers should seek their own legal advice or help from qualified professionals for any rage disorder, road rage accident, or other driving related need. The information in this book should be read with the understanding that the information contained herein is for entertainment value only. Those who wish to view the material in this book as anything other than entertainment should contact the publisher for a full refund (purchase price) upon return of the book to the publisher.

Cover design by Studio WD

Library of Congress LCCN Data
McKay, Gary E.
    Road rage - commuter combat in America/Gary E. McKay 1st ed.

    Includes bibliographical references and index.
    ISBN 0-9675639-0-9

Edited by Dick Hursey, Ph.D.   **LCCN: 00 131451**

About the Author

Gary McKay has authored several books and published a number of articles on subjects such as e-mail, diet drugs, road rage, the great outdoors, and the environment.

He has an extensive safety background in nuclear weapons, civilian nuclear power generation, management of environmental cleanup projects, people management, and other highly technical areas, which allows him to understand and write about the complex issues that face us today from a unique perspective. During a twelve year period, from 1988 to 2000, he logged over 600,000 commuter miles behind the wheel while studying road rage.

He resides in rural Missouri with his wife, Lori, and three of their six children.

Acknowledgement

To my wife, Lori. Without her steadfast love and support this book would not have been possible. Thanks for keeping the kids quiet, for being patient over the long nights I spent banging away at the keyboard, and for believing in me. God doesn't make them any better than you.

Dedicated to Jennifer Lynn Hywari

Born: August 30, 1974
Died: August 11, 1997

And

Matthew Warren Jones
Born: February 9, 1978
Died: December 31, 1999

May you both rest in God's peace and love.

Table of Contents

Part One:	The Tragic Stories	13

Chapter One: **A Deadly Morning Commute**   15
- A Soul goes to Heaven   18
- Life Goes On   19
- Katie   21
- The 8:00 News   22

Chapter Two: **Little White Crosses:**   25
Saying Goodbye to Jennifer
- Her Name was Jennifer   27
- Jennettie's Little Girl   27
- Grief Classes   29
- The Conviction of   30
  John Devanny
- Princess Diana Dies   33
- Taking Action   34
- Fifteen Minutes of Fame   37

Chapter Three: **Brake Slamming**   39
- Madman in a Pickup Truck   40
- Fireman Hits the Brakes   42
- Brakes Slam, A Fetus Dies   43
- A Rodeo Clown   44
  Slams em' Down

Chapter Four: **Forcing Other Drivers Off the**   45
Road and Vehicle Ramming
- 23 Seniors Die in Bus Crash   45
- The Driver's Ed. Teacher   46
- Toyota takes on Semi: 47
  Toyota Loses
- Vehicle Rammings   47
- A Broken Back   48
- A Freeway Joust Ends   48
  in Death
- Family of Four Forced   48
  off the Road
- You're Not Going to   49
  Pass Me! - Five Die

Table of Contents

Chapter Five:	Roadside Stabbings, Beatings, Assaults	51
	- Stoplight Stabbing - (An Old Vigilante)	52
	- Get Out of My Way!	53
	- Older Driver Beaten Unconscious	53
	- The Professor and the DEA Agent	54
	- Mike Tyson Attacks	56
	- Cab Driver Kicks Pregnant Woman	57
	- The Knife and the Pit Bull	57
	- Face Slashed with Garden Shears	58
	- Elderly man Attacked and Killed	58
	- Teen is Killed in Road Attack	59
	- Attacked Woman Jumps from Bridge	60

Chapter Six:	Shootings on the Highway	61
	- Timmy Scully is Gunned Down	62
	- Laura MacPhee is Shot and Killed	63
	- Father's Road Rage Kills His own Son	65

Chapter Seven:	Big-Rig Rage: Attacked by an 18-Wheeler	67
	- Three Teens Run Over by Semi	68
	- An Enraged Truck Driver	69
	- A Short Cut	71
	- Real-Life Horror Flick	72
	- Staring Death in the Face	73
	- Get Away from Michael!	75
	- Attempted Murder	76
	- Prelude to Disaster	78
	- Lessons Learned	85
	- Semi Runs over Sleeping Camper	86
	- A Jealous Rage	86
	- Campground Shoot-Out	87

Table of Contents

Chapter Eight: **Random Acts of Road Rage**   89
- *Road Rage in Peoria*   89
- *Officer Assaulted with Tomatoes*   90
- *Minivan-vs.-Suburban*   92
- *Pepper Mace and Ramming Kills two*   92
- *Disabled Man & Son Beaten*   94
- *The Crossbow Church Deacon*   95
- *Sara and Leo*   95

Chapter Nine: **Under Attack: Bicyclists**   99
- *London England Woman Runs Down Cyclist*   101
- *Bad Cyclists*   103
- *Biking Can be Dangerous*   104
- *Many Cities Opt for Bike Lanes*   105

Chapter Ten: **The Amish Under Attack**   107
- *Men Attack Amish Cyclists with Tire Irons*   108
- *Professor Bryan Byers*   109
- *Buggy Bashing*   110
- *Horse Riders Being Assaulted*   112

Chapter Eleven: **Highway Workers Attacked**   113
- *Highway Worker Faces Ax Attack*   113
- *Some Workers are Killed*   114
- *"My Orange Vest was Ripped from my Back"*   115
- *Assaulted with Flying Objects*   115

Part Two: **The Many Causes Of Road Rage**   117

Chapter Twelve: **NHTSA**   119
- *The Experts Speak Out*   121
- *Definitions of Aggressive Driving Vary*   123
- *Causes*   124
- *An International Problem*   126
- *Ongoing Research*   126

Chapter Thirteen: **The Road Rage Detail**   129
- *The Illinois State Police Fight Back*   129

Table of Contents

Chapter Thirteen (cont.)	- *Impressive Statistics*	131
	- *A Typical Road Rage Profile*	133
	- *Those Who Drive too Slow*	134
	- *Cell Phones*	135
	- *A Ride in a Stealth Police Car*	136
	- *A Layman's Analysis*	142
	- *Never Give an Inch*	145
	- *Four Troopers Run Over In Indiana*	146
Chapter Fourteen:	**The Pressures of Today**	147
	- *Many Factors*	148
	- *Tailgating*	152
	- *Losing Your Head*	152
	- *A Rock and Roll Load*	154
	- *The Passing Lane*	154
	- *The Baby Sitter*	156
	- *The Foreign Driver*	160
	- *The Melting Pot*	164
	- *Isolationism*	166
	- *Longer Work Hours, Less Time Off*	167
	- *The Japan Factor*	169
Chapter Fifteen:	**Bad Roads, Bridges, and Highways**	173
	- *The Gasoline Tax*	174
	- *The Trip Report*	174
	- *The 'Road to Hell'*	175
Part Three:	**The Keys to Highway Survival**	179
Chapter Sixteen:	**Understanding the Modern Truck Driver**	181
	- *Nuclear Missiles*	182
	- *Sharing the Road*	183
	- *Dramatic Increases in Trucking Activity*	184
	- *Accident Statistics*	185
	- *Get Out of the Way*	186
	- *When are you Coming Home Dad?*	187
	- *Impossible Deadlines*	188
	- *A Severe Shortage of Drivers*	191
	- *Lumping*	193
	- *A Need for Compassion*	194

Table of Contents

Chapter Seventeen: **Curbing the Mile-High Menace**   197

- *Road Rage Getting Worse?*   198
- *Public Awareness*   199
  Campaigns
- *Smile, You're on Van-did*   200
  Camera
- *Unnecessary Deaths*   200
- *Increase in Aggressive*   201
  Driving is Measurable
- *Demographics*   204

Chapter Eighteen: **The UK and other Countries**   207
Fight Road Rage

Chapter Nineteen: **A Few Personal Notes on**   209
Road Rage

- *A Saturday from Hell*   209
- *A Little Side Errand*   211
- *A Final Word*   214
- *Protecting Yourself*   215
- *Self Control and*   215
  Confrontations
- *The Middle Third*   216

Reference Section   217

Index   219

Footnotes   221

The Cover

On July 14, 1999, a Seattle, Washington, man was severely beaten with a baseball bat after a road rage confrontation on Mercer Island. The attack occurred during rush hour traffic.

The victim, Chris Grasser, 22 years old, suffered a fractured skull and a concussion.[1]

As of this writing, his attacker has not been found...

(Photo is a representation only and not physically related to this case)

Foreward... ... ...

Road Rage. Millions of us have been bombarded with this catchy sound bite for a number of years, now. We hear it everywhere. Some have used it to draw attention to their causes. Politicians have used it to scare up more federal dollars for programs. Some in our society have grown to hate the phrase, condemning it as too "sensational" or claiming that it draws attention away from their particular cause.

So successful and "descriptive" is the phrase, "road rage," that it has spilled over into other areas. Air rage, phone rage, workplace rage, spousal rage, computer rage, and on and on. Truth is, like a stroke of Madison Avenue advertising genius, the term, road rage, *sells*. It hits hard. And to the point. But why? I believe the answer is simple. We all know instantly what it means. No further explanation is required. Why? Simply put, most of us have either experienced it firsthand, have been guilty of committing it sometime in our driving history, or know someone who has had a close call or been injured or killed by an enraged driver.

The term, road rage, draws attention to the violent acts being committed on our roads, and I use it without hesitation. It does not matter to me whether the road rage driver is an angry drunk, a ticked-off druggie, or a sober but mad-at-the-world housewife. It has helped get the message out about this horrendous scourge.

It is my hope that this book will help in the fight against road rage and death on our highways. More Americans are killed on our roads than by any other cause or occupation. Let the carnage stop.

Rage: *"To be violently angry...to move with deadly force"*

Part One

The Tragic Stories

In Part One, we take a close look at just a handful of road rage stories that have occurred over the last few years. While researching stories for this book, I was overwhelmed by the shear number of tragic stories across the U.S. and around the world. There is no way to capture them all. No single book could contain the shear volume needed to capture the thousands of tragic deaths, beatings, shootings, car rammings, and other rage filled acts that are being carried out on our roadways every day. Some of the stories chronicled in this book have made national headlines. While the most graphic and spectacularly evil stories may be deemed newsworthy by the media, my research uncovered literally hundreds of untold road rage incidents. There is little doubt in my mind that *thousands* of road rage stories will never be told. Telephone calls to sheriff's departments, highway patrol offices, and other law enforcement agencies across the nation revealed countless roadway incidents where rage played a part in these tragic deaths and crippling encounters on our roadways. It seemed like every officer had a number of harrowing stories to tell, most of them recent.

However, by my telling a few stories here, maybe the reader will get some idea of how dangerous our roadways have become. By digging a little deeper than the sound bite headlines splashed across the pages of our newspapers, we find stories that take us into the lives of both the victims and their attackers. These stories give us new insight into just how terribly vicious it can get out there on our roads. Any road. And in the time span of just a few seconds. A peaceful drive, even to the corner drug store, can turn deadly in an instant.

Read on, and as you read, try to place yourself in the shoes of the victims. The shoes of the family members who survive and try to live on and cope.

Chapter One

A Deadly Morning Commute

There was nothing unusual about my commute that morning. The same 65 miles one way, over the same back roads and across the same three crowded highways. It was a muggy morning, typical for mid-August in Missouri. The kind of morning when you find yourself a little less cheery than normal. It was August 11, 1997. The morning air was already a thick 70 degrees at 7:00 am. The high that day would reach 92 hot Midwestern degrees. This was the kind of sultry summer day that worries police agencies the most, for they know that when the temperatures soar, so do tempers. *Especially for those who work outside in the heat. They know they're headed for a long, rough day on mornings like that one.* But at least the driving conditions on this particular morning were pleasant, with not a cloud in the sky.

As usual, I had left the house earlier than most to avoid the worst of the traffic jams. In the seven years since I had moved back to St. Louis with my lovely new bride and family, the traffic jams had gone from occasionally bad to *"Look out L.A., you've got competition!"*

Leaving the house early for work and heading for home a little earlier (or a lot later) than most commuters was my only hope of beating the "highway hordes." If you tarry in the morning and hit the road too late, the lane darters, speeding tailgaters, red light runners, angry middle-finger flickers, and other highway acrobats will be out en masse.

I had come to realize that leaving home just 20 or 30 minutes later than my usual departure time could cost me hours on the road sitting in endless stop-and-go misery. The same rule applied to the return trip home.

A Fatal Car Crash

I had managed to get an early start and the drivers on both northbound Highway 55 and Highway 270 had been exceptionally civil this particular morning. The other early bird commuters seemed to be in the same spirit. *Just take it easy, and we'll all get there, folks.* It's like that nowadays, you know. You really notice when drivers, for some unexplained reason, all seem to be behaving themselves. Too bad.

I made it to the Highway 40 interchange, *the last leg of my usual morning trip*, in good time and headed west toward Weldon Spring. As I topped the hill near Chesterfield Mall, I saw the traffic ahead coming to a stop. You can always count on light westbound Highway 40 traffic in the morning, so I knew the accident somewhere ahead was most likely a bad one.

There were police and fire crews everywhere. More emergency vehicles than you would normally see handling a highway accident. The eastbound lanes had been completely shut down, and there seemed to be people milling about everywhere.

Some drivers had left their cars and were standing around in small groups. Some were crying, head in hands, still others were holding on to each other. Whatever had happened here had been traumatic. Most highway accidents are, but this one seemed worse than most.

> "...You can always count on light westbound Highway 40 traffic in the morning, so I knew the accident somewhere ahead was most likely a bad one."

A Soul Goes to Heaven

As the line of cars ahead slowly rolled closer to the accident scene, I could see that there was little doubt as to the outcome of this one. This poor soul never had a chance.

I could see the car clearly, and I had seen this kind of accident more than once before. There was little doubt that the mid-sized car had flipped and rolled at least a few times. There was a partially covered body lying on the roadway. Someone had just died a sudden and horrific death.

The tractor-trailer rig, however, seemed to have sustained little, if any, damage. Was the rig involved at all? Even the semi's I had seen in head-on collisions always sustained at least *some* damage. Maybe one of the vehicles had swerved into the damaged car while going the same direction? Maybe another car had been involved in the accident. But if so, where was it? How could it have been hauled away so quickly? This accident scene somehow seemed very different.

I whispered a silent prayer to myself for the family of the dead as the traffic sped up again and I drove away. To this day, I can still see the body, partially covered by a white sheet and surrounded by a small army of police and emergency medical personnel. It was obvious that a life had come to a terrible, violent end amidst a tangle of steel, glass, and rubber. *A terrible and sad waste of life.*

Life Goes On

Now well past the accident, the pace quickens again, and so I speed up to match the traffic flow *and avoid getting run over.* Continuing on to work, only now deep in thought, I unconsciously find myself driving a little slower the rest of the way.

I've only traveled a mile or so from the accident, and traffic has once again sped up to the usual feverish pace. Such is the habit of the traffic masses. Once beyond the delay, once beyond the inconvenience, the momentary aggravation, life speeds up again...life goes on.

The traffic delay had taken only 10, maybe 15 minutes, but commuters' schedules have been upset. *The lost time must be recovered.*

I'm one-and-a-half miles away now, and several commuters speed past me as though I were sitting still. Determination. Drive. Career. Something seems to be driving us all. *Onward. Faster. Colder.* Conditioned to the scene just past as if it was only a Hollywood movie. Someone else's tears. Someone else's loss. The other guy's pain. We have our own problems.

Mile two: a young man rumbles past me on the left. I can't help but notice the baseball cap turned backwards and screwed down tightly on his skull-shaved head, his smashed ears jutting out like Yoda in Star Wars.

I can't help but notice too, his animated head bobbing up and down and side to side to the beat of the music. The bass on his stereo, turned up to an ear-shattering level, reverberates as he passes. His focus is seemingly on anything but the road ahead and the safety or the rights of other travelers. The fatal accident is just behind us. Is he totally blind to what has just happened?

Again, I can't help but notice the cold stare in his eyes and the slight grin as he flies past. *At least he doesn't flip me off for doing just 65 mph in a 60 mph zone. A cardinal sin to some, to be sure, and a sure fire cause for middle-fingered reprisal most mornings.* Obviously, the fatal accident scene he had just driven past hadn't phased him in the least. He was too busy being too cool...Is this a time to laugh? My God, what's going on here?

A Time to Think

I get to the parking lot safe and sound. From years of habit, I park in the same spot. *Being creatures of habit, we usually do that.* I get out of my truck and head for the same door I've opened for almost seven years.

Still deep in thought, the highway death scene only moments past, I notice little around me. I walk head down, in deep reflection. How firm the pavement is. How convenient for modern travel. How unforgiving of human flesh and bone.

Someone won't be showing up for work today. There will be an empty space in some parking lot this morning. A mother or father has lost a child. A child a parent. A lover will mourn for beauty lost. Beauty wasted. Children never born.

The *conscious few* among those who saw this terrible accident will hold their loved ones a little tighter tonight...a little longer, too.

Katie......

Katie is a good hearted person. Always cheerful, seldom down. Always helpful and courteous, she's one of those bubbly people who just by their contagious nature help others get through their troubled day. But not this morning.

I have yet to set my briefcase down when I overhear her talking with a coworker about the accident. Katie, too, had seen the wreck. Distraught, she is vivid and animated as she speaks. Using her hands, clutching her face, she struggles to shape the words properly. She is visibly shaken. Almost to tears. With a tinny, quivering, shallow voice, she manages to get the words to come out.

"So, you saw that bad accident on Highway 40, too, Katie?" I ask.

"Yeah, I saw it happen. It happened right in front of me," she says. "Some guy pulled in front of this lady and slammed on his brakes. She swerved to avoid hitting him and lost control. I saw the car cross the median and begin to roll. The lady came flying out of her car and a car ran right over her. It ran right over her! I can't believe what I just saw. My god, I can't believe it. She never had a chance. That poor driver! That poor lady!"

I ask her if she's OK. She nods yes and walks off with another woman, mumbling under her breath, fighting her emotions, trying to cope with the pictures running through her mind.

Other cube dwellers start to file in now. The late-comers are arriving. With each one, the routine is the same. They each stick their head in my office and exclaim, "Wow, did you see..." "Yeah, I saw the accident right after it happened.

Katy saw the whole thing happen right in front of her. She's pretty shook up," I respond.

The Evening Dinner Table.........

"Honey, did you hear what happened on Highway 40 this morning?" my wife, Lori, asks.

"Yea, Babe, I saw it. I also heard it on KMOX on the way home," I respond. "They say some guy got mad at her and ran her off the road. It's getting meaner all the time out there."

"Dad, why would someone do something so terrible?" Scotty, my inquisitive eight-year-old, asks. "How could anybody kill someone by running them off the road like that?"

I swallow hard, as fathers do with such tough questions from little boys. "I don't know Buddy...I guess they just get mad and don't think about what they're doing," I respond weakly. For a moment, he stares back at me in silence, his little expression signaling his still unsatisfied need to understand.

Just what do you say to an eight year old boy about something like this? How can he possibly understand? Rational words that his little mind could possibly absorb fail me at times like that.

The 8:00 O' Clock News

"In tonight's top news story, St. Louis County Police report a bizarre twist in the gruesome fatal accident that killed a 22-year-old woman this morning. The accident occurred on Highway 40, just west of Chesterfield Mall, during the morning rush hour. The victim's name is being withheld pending notification of relatives.

"Reportedly, police say that when a man, allegedly 27-year-old John Devanny, approached the crash scene and offered to help, witnesses to the crash recognized him as the driver of the small truck that had slammed on its brakes and caused her to lose control.

"Several of the witnesses apparently pointed him out saying, '*That's him! He's the guy who slammed his brakes on in front of her!*' Police then took Devanny into custody. He is being held in the St. Louis County Jail, pending arraignment on charges of vehicular manslaughter and possibly murder."

Chapter Two

Little White Crosses - Saying Goodbye to Jennifer

For two years now I've driven past her two symbolic graves, one on the westbound shoulder, the other on the eastbound side of Highway 40, through what is known as Chesterfield Valley in West St. Louis County. The graves are marked with little white crosses which read simply, "Jennifer Hywari, 8-11-97." They mark the spot where, on that fateful morning, 22-year-old Jennifer, instantly terrified by a road rage attack, lost control of her vehicle, crossed the median, and died.

And for two years, now, thousands of commuters like me have been reminded daily of that tragic morning when a lovely young lady lost her life to a rage filled young man. An angry man who had been delayed. Someone was in his way. Someone had slowed him down. Caused him to spill his coffee.

Not a workday goes by that I don't see those symbolic graves along the highway and think about that terrible morning. I hope many others do, too, including John Devanny

I was prompted, no, *driven,* to write this book because of Jennifer. I never knew her. Neither did Katie, Curt, or the dozens of others I worked with at the time, who passed by the wreckage and Jennifer's lifeless body that morning. Nor did the thousands of our fellow commuters who pass by her symbolic memorial graves each day. Yet, somehow I feel the loss. Maybe Katie and Curt do, too. For thousands of St. Louisans, this single tragic event is forever etched into our memories.

But there is also an opposite truth: for sure, *many drivers could care less.* To them, the symbolic graves must be by now just another road sign. No different than a mile marker, *a "McDonald's, Next Exit"* sign. It must be that way. Why do I say this?

Well, I still see drivers giving the finger. I still see impatience almost every day and sometimes anger on that very same stretch of road. People still slam on their brakes. They tailgate, weaving and swerving wildly in and out of traffic. Many get a belly laugh out of it. Others scream, threaten, and intimidate at will.

To gain a better perspective of the aftermath of these sometimes horrific road rage tragedies, let's take a closer look at this single story. Jennifer's story.

Her Name was Jennifer

One of the main objectives of this book is to prompt the reader to an understanding of the immediate human tragedy that can result from road rage and aggressive driving. You will also get a glimpse into the utter heartbreak, pain, and loneliness of the survivors. The human aftermath of road rage.

As the rest of the world goes about its business, not missing a beat, *those left behind often live the rest of their lives in quiet desperation.*

A Visit with Jennifer's Parents

My wife, Lori, and I visited Jennifer's mother and stepfather, Mike and Jennettie Lierman, on June 15, 1998, not quite a year after Jennifer's death. They live in a nice middle-class home nestled just across the street from a large park graced by large mature live oaks. Children were playing when we arrived.

Jennettie's Little Girl

Jennifer Hywari was more than a statistic. She was Jennettie Lierman's baby girl. Only a mother who has carried a baby in her womb for nine wonderful months, gone through the trials of giving birth, and then held that little miracle in her arms knows the bond between a mother and child.

Jennifer was also Jennettie's *only child.*

She was Jennettie's inquisitive 5, 8, and 12, year-old. As we speak softly at her kitchen table, she gently remembers how Jennifer was her sanity when things got tough. "She was my best friend," Jennettie says. "We went through a lot together. We went through some real tough times, and got through it by leaning on each other. We were very close. She was my best friend in the whole world. I never imagined that I would ever lose her," she continues.

Jennifer was also Jennettie's tough, often stubborn teenager. As most parents know, there is certainly nothing unusual about that. However, it is that same stubbornness that can enable a growing young boy or girl to say "no" to drugs, "no" to early sex and other unwise things. It can give them the tenacity to accomplish great things in life, too. According to her mother, Jennifer was on her way to doing just that before she was killed on that summer morning. She possessed an appreciation and zest for life that was contagious.

"Jennifer was very smart," said Jennettie. "I knew she was very special from the beginning. She loved life and was cheerful most of the time. Everyone seemed to like her a lot, especially kids. She just loved children. She would play with them in the park across the street. She had collected over 300 Snoopy's. She just loved Snoopy. She was also a major hockey fan."

(Jennifer was buried with one of her Snoopy's and a Philadelphia Flyers jersey, her favorite team).

And she had made Mike and Jennettie proud as a successful 22-year-old college graduate. It had been hard for her, but her determination and loving support from Jennettie and Mike had gotten her through. "It was tough for her, but she did it," said Mike. "We were very proud." Jennifer had graduated with a degree in history and had made the dean's list. She also loved the opera, French, and

Slurpees. She had planned to attend the University of Missouri at St. Louis, to work toward her MBA in business while working full time. Jennifer had been out of her parents' home and on her own for just three weeks, testing her independent wings when she was killed on that fateful August morning.

She was on her way to work as a temporary employee for Nelcor Puritan Bennet Company as a medical marketing coordinator. "She liked her job and was hoping to get hired full time soon. She was really hopeful. Things seemed to be looking up for her," said Jennettie.

Jennifer was Mike's joy too. Immediately upon hearing him speak, Lori and I sensed the caring, quiet dignity in his nature. Jennifer must have loved him very much.

A quiet, gentle man, Mike suffers from the loss of his beloved stepdaughter daily. *This author, himself the step father of two girls and a boy, all of them healthy, high-spirited teenagers now, knows just how close a step family can become.*

Jennettie and Mike talk of the crash, the long-awaited trial, and the day her attacker, John Devanny, was finally sentenced. Although they have suffered through a great deal, their poise and self-control is amazing.

Grief Classes

One of the things Mike and Jennettie spoke of during our visit was their grief classes. Mike explained how they attend the classes at a local hospital two or three times a week. "Because of my job, I go to the afternoon sessions and Jennettie goes in the mornings. At the classes, we sit and talk with others who have lost loved ones. It has helped us a lot. It's a great support group." (Mike attended the classes for about a year after the crash. Jennettie still attends once a week).

"I tell people I have an angel for a daughter, now," says Jennettie.

While researching for this book, I spoke with Ms. Lisa Jones, who serves on the St. Louis County Prosecuting Attorney's "Victim Service Council." Her job involves helping victims and families of victims of violent crimes. "Mike and Jennettie are wonderful people," Ms. Jones comments. "I told them that if Jennifer's death results in causing people to think twice about aggressive driving, retaliating on the highway, and other dangerous behavior, then she will not have died in vain."

We talk a while longer with Mike and Jennettie, and as we head for the door to leave, they show us pictures of Jennifer on their living room wall near the front door. A simple, pictorial shrine to their beloved daughter.

Fighting our own emotions, we say good-bye and begin to head for our car. Jennettie leaves us with: "You know, I feel a lot better about this now." Obviously, she was concerned about how the story will be told. Would it be told at all? Are we just another couple of media-hyping nuts, or are we serious about helping to stop road rage and telling Jennifer's story?

The Conviction of John Devanny

John Devanny was a self-employed roofer with a history of speeding tickets and moving violations, according to newspaper reports.[2] On at least two prior occasions, he had had his license revoked or suspended. It was also reported that Devanny once had a protective court order filed against him by a former girlfriend.

In the petition, she said that he had become violent on more than one occasion, and during one fit of rage, had slammed her against his truck. Apparently, he had a short fuse long before encountering Jennifer on that fateful morning.

After the accident, he had returned to the scene and pretended to be a witness to the event. However, several witnesses recognized him as the driver of the truck involved. Devanny was arrested and released on $25,000 bond. He was later indicted by a St Louis grand jury on involuntary manslaughter charges.

During the trial, Devanny admitted having spilled hot coffee on himself while driving his red Toyota pickup and braking behind Jennifer as she drove her black Ford Tempo westbound on highway 40. Jennifer was apparently driving too slow in the passing lane, at least from DeVanny's point of view. (Although she was doing near the speed limit and could not get over fast enough due to traffic.) He admitted pulling around beside her and giving an obscene gesture, then pulling in front of her and slamming on his brakes, causing her to lose control of her car as she fought to avoid hitting him.

According to the prosecuting attorney, Mike Archer, the fact that there was no traffic ahead of Devanny when he got around Jennifer played a big role in his conviction. After he had passed her, he could have driven away unimpeded. However, he chose rather to "show her a thing or two." His actions demonstrated a clear choice on his part: revenge.

On April 9, 1998, John Devanny was found guilty of involuntary manslaughter and sentenced to five years in the Algoa Correctional Facility at Jefferson City, Missouri. He waived appeal and asked to be sentenced immediately for his crime. At his sentencing, Devanny broke down in tears, and standing next to Jennettie at a microphone, expressed his sorrow for Jennifer's death.

"I can't justify my actions," Devanny said. "But I have to live with this the rest of my life. I'm a working man and I have a family, and I love my family with all my heart. I hope other people who live around here can learn from this, learn that cars are weapons. I never set out that morning to hurt anybody. As God is my witness, I love my fellow man."

Incredibly, Jennettie, with more grace than most of us could possibly hope to muster, held his hand, embraced him, and told him that she believed that he had acted out of anger. "I believe in my heart that you were a very angry person that morning. I also believe that whatever angered you that morning had nothing to do with my daughter, and my daughter paid the price for it. I believe you are sincere. But she was the love of my life, and this trial today has not brought closure for me," Jennettie said.

Many in the media and those of us watching at home, took this moment when they held hands to mean that Jennettie had forgiven Devanny for causing her daughter's death. "We want to make it clear," Mike Lierman later told me over the phone, "that Jennettie has not forgiven him. What she said that day was that *she truly believed he was sorry*. That's not the same as forgiveness. She basically felt his pain that day. That doesn't change how she feels about what he *did*. She wants him to serve out his sentence. This guy took Jennifer's life. Jennettie's only daughter. How can she forgive that?"

I later attempted to interview John Devanny at the prison. He refused to be interviewed.

Princess Diana Dies -
Just Weeks after Jennifer

Just a few weeks after Jennifer Hywari was killed, the entire world cried together when Princess Diana was killed in a terrible car crash in Paris, France. Yet, we never knew her *personally.*

Her beauty, her caring heart, her love for her two young boys, even her flaws and mistakes, endeared her to our hearts. No phony aristocrat here. She was the real stuff. A lot like us.

Her entire adult life played out in front of us as we watched her from afar. We overlooked her mistakes and forgave her faults. Many of us saw ourselves in her. She was real; no fake smiles here. Although awash in royalty and splendor, she was, or so it seemed, the common man's type of princess. She made the world a better place while she was on earth.

It has been said that many of us *"live lives of quiet desperation."* Surely, this is true. For the lucky among us, though, very special, beautiful people enter our lives, making life worth living. They bring special moments of joy to our hearts and fill us with their energy, their zest, and their contagious love for life.

Princess Diana was like that. *Jennifer Hywari was like that, too.* We didn't know her either, but she was a lot like Princess Diana. Though worlds apart in fame and fortune, both were vibrant women, unafraid to take on the world.

Sadly, though, they did share a few things in common in their deaths:

Princess Diana's accident didn't have to happen. It was avoidable. Jennifer's accident didn't have to happen, either. It, too, was avoidable.

Princess Diana was killed by another driver's hands. Jennifer was, too.

Today, thousands flock to see Princess Diana's gravesite and her childhood home at Althorp Mansion in England. And today, thousands drive by Jennifer's gravesite memorials along Highway 40, west of St. Louis.

To her friends in the smaller, more peaceful world in which she lived, to her coworkers and especially to Jennettie and Mike, Jennifer was *their princess.* Just like your child may be a little princess or prince to you. If you have children, you surely know what I mean.

Taking Action

Today, Jennettie and Mike Lierman speak to thousands of students and adults in schools, colleges, newspapers, and on TV and radio talk shows about the dangers of road rage. They work through an organization called The Partnership for Safe Driving, with headquarters in Washington, DC. You will find the e-mail address and those of other prevention groups listed in the back of this book.

Jennettie and Mike's strength and courage undoubtedly inspire all those who hear them speak.

Why don't we care? What is happening to our roads and highways? *Our people?* That's what I set out to unravel when I began to write this book. We owe it to Jennifer. We owe it to ourselves. We also owe it to the next generation. Our kids.

Experts can argue for many years to come about just who was at fault in Princess Diana's death. Was it the drunk driver? The paparazzi? (Though they were later exonerated and the driver blamed.) Was it, as some claim, the millions of admirers who wanted to know more, see more, hear more about her, causing her to become depressed because she lacked privacy? Regardless, she is gone forever, and two beautiful boys have forever lost their mother. A family has lost a sister, a daughter, a dear friend.

Experts can argue about Jennifer's death, too. She should have done this. He said he didn't mean to do that, etc. No matter. None of the speculation will bring her back to Jennettie and Mike. She's gone. Forever.

All across this great land, there are deeply wounded survivors who will never fully heal. Children once dreamed of never to be born. Hopes of grandchildren vanquished forever.

There are silent, empty bedrooms like Jennifer's, once filled with the laughter of a child, now solemn shrines in memory of a lost loved one. A favorite pipe will go un-smoked by a father, a favorite TV program will go unwatched. A caregiver for an elderly mother or father will be killed, leaving a dependant elderly person to wilt and die for lack of care.

The anguish of such a loss, even of just one family member, is magnified many times over. Despair ripples through family, friends, coworkers, and the community.

Even in Death, Jennifer Helped 50 People

In death, as during her life, Jennifer helped others. According to her mother, Jennifer had insisted on being an organ donor.

Following her death, two people received her eyes. Someone got her heart valves. Others received her skin (burn victims), and on and on. *More than 50 in all*...and just as she would want it, some children, whom she dearly loved, also received her gifts of life.

Update: John Devanny was up for parole in October 1998, only six months after going to prison. At the parole hearing, Devanny reportedly denied any responsibility for Jennifer's death, according to Jennettie. He never looked at the victim's family and blamed the entire event on Jennifer. His parole was denied.

Devanny will be released to travel our highways again in April 2001. He will be on probation until August 2003. According to the prison psychiatrist, he is not receiving any kind of anger therapy. Jennettie was told that with over 2,500 prisoners, there are not enough resources for individual treatment.

In the summer of 1999, Jennettie Lierman helped pass a new aggressive driving law, Ordanance No. 19,508 in St. Louis County. On the first day it became law, a driver cut another off in St. Louis County and was followed for 15 miles. When the first driver stopped in a hospital parking lot, the pursuer jumped out with a golf club and began smashing the other driver's windshield. Police responded and issued him a ticket for aggressive driving.

The following poem, was written by Jennifer Hywari before she died. The words she penned here, seemingly wise beyond her years, would come to represent the prophetic foretelling of the tragic end of her own life. Her fifteen minutes of fame, as her poem says, *did her no good.* Just maybe, though, her words here will help someone else.

We will never know what beauty Jennettie's little girl could have brought the world:

Fifteen Minutes

Does everyone really get
Fifteen minutes to shine?
Haven't seen anyone
It was actually good for.

I wonder what mine will be -
A discovery that will change the world?
A torrid love affair?
A scandal in Washington?

With any luck, it'll be much worse.
Because for those fifteen minutes
Everyone will know me.

Jennifer Hywari
Born: August 30, 1974
Died: August 11, 1997

Chapter Three

Brake Slamming

Brake slamming appears to be a favorite among road ragers. During the last nine years, I've seen this happen on the highways in and around St. Louis on a number of occasions, and once had it happen to me. To this day, I'm not sure what I did to tick off the other driver, but to be sure, this author had a close call. From the look in his eyes, he may have been on drugs, have been drinking, or maybe he was just mean. One thing is for sure, whether he was under some kind of influence or not, he was an extremely enraged man. Here's what happened.

Madman in a Pickup Truck

Several years ago, I was travelling south on Interstate 55 just south of St. Louis. I was heading home from work. It was a typical summer's day with nothing unusual in the works. Just a long string of commuters heading home.

I came up behind a slow moving tractor-trailer rig in the right lane. I looked in my mirror and saw that the coast was clear, so I began to ease around the truck in the left lane.

I was nearly clear of the truck and preparing to pull back into the right lane when out of nowhere appeared an older model Chevy pickup in my rear-view mirror. The driver was waving his fist frantically and screaming. He must have been doing at least 90 and was right on top of me.

I put my turn signal on and moved over into the right lane, but it was already too late. This driver was enraged and tried to swerve his truck into my Ford F-150. He then pulled in front of me and slammed on his brakes. I swerved back into the left lane to avoid hitting him. He then pulled in front of me again in the left lane and hit his brakes again. This went back and forth several times, until I finally pulled over onto the shoulder. In my mirrors, I could see that the traffic behind us had nearly come to a complete stop. Wisely, the truck driver had watched the whole scene in front of him and was straddling the lanes and slowing down the traffic.

The beat-up old pickup truck stopped in front of me momentarily, then sped off, throwing gravel. I sat there for a while, my nerves shot. I didn't know if he was going to get out and put a bullet into my head or what. I've never seen the truck or the driver again.

So you don't think it's getting meaner out there? If so, what planet have you been living on?

The only explanation I can come up with, is that I was just the unfortunate one who had been in his way. He was an enraged man and was looking for trouble. The following victim had an experience similar to mine. She too, was lucky enough to walk away.

Minnetonka, Minnesota
Brake Slamming Victim Gets Lucky

Catherine Costello, 36, of Minnetonka, Minnesota, also knows what it's like to be a victim of a road rage brake slammer. In the spring of 1997, she reported the following incident to the Minnesota State Patrol.[3]

Ms. Costello was driving on Interstate 494 in her Honda Civic when a black Mercedes came up fast behind her. "I pulled to the right lane hoping he would go around me," Ms. Costello said. "Instead, he pulled into the right lane, right behind me."

She then tapped her brakes (as Jennifer Hywari had done) but to no avail. He stayed right on her rear bumper. She then pumped her brakes, and he continued to stay on her tail.

Moments later, the Mercedes driver pulled alongside her, looked at her with a laugh, and raced to get ahead of her. Then, just as John Devanny had done to Jennifer Hywari, the Mercedes driver pulled in front of Ms. Costello and slammed on his brakes. She locked up her brakes and skidded to a complete stop to avoid hitting him. Luckily, she escaped injury. Later, she said she was so upset she "couldn't function at work."

Ms. Costello was very lucky indeed. It is not advisable to tap your brakes to try and fend off a tailgater. Let them get around you or pull over, but don't provoke a violent response by hitting your brakes. You don't know who that person is, and they could have a deadly mind for all you know. You might also cause a deadly accident yourself, albeit unintentional.

Fireman Hits the Brakes

On September 10, 1999, fireman Daniel Denny, a 30 year Phoenix Fire Department veteran, was arrested for allegedly causing a road rage incident on the Loop 101 Aqua Fria Freeway near 35th street in Phoenix, Arizona.[4]

According to police accounts, Denny became enraged at the driver of a BMW as they traveled eastbound. The BMW was apparently in the fast lane. Denny apparently crowded the BMW until the driver moved over.

When the BMW pulled behind him, Denny reportedly slammed on his brakes causing the BMW driver to lose control and cross into the west bound lanes. The BMW hit two cars in the oncoming lanes, and five cars hit debris from the wreck.

Denny was found two days later after a license plate check identified him as the suspect they were looking for. He was arrested on one count of aggravated assault, eight counts of criminal damage, and three counts of endangerment.

As of this writing, the charges were still pending.

Brakes Slam, a Fetus Dies

In a much celebrated case back in 1996, Tracie Alfieri, of Mt. Washington, Ohio, was convicted of hitting her brakes in front of Rene Andrews, causing her to crash. Mrs. Andrews was seriously injured and subsequently lost her unborn baby boy. Ms. Alfieri was charged under Ohio's new fetal-protection law that allows people to be tried for criminal manslaughter or murder for causing the death of a fetus.[5]

At her sentencing on May 25, 1999, in an ironic twist, Alfieri was only given five years probation and a $100 fine. The light sentence was apparently due to the fact that Ms. Alfieri had to take care of her disabled child, who was three years old and suffering from brain damage after the removal of a tumor. The child had the tumor removed while Alfieri was awaiting trial. She also was required to perform 100 hours of community service and had her license suspended for three years.

At the sentencing, Mrs. Andrews stated that she and her husband had been unable to have another child, and she blamed the accident for it. Ms. Alfieri's actions caused another mother to lose her child, yet she was set free to care for her own.

A Rodeo Clown Slams 'em Down

On September 11, 1999, 21-year old Shaun Mohr of Cincinnati was southbound on Interstate 275 with his girl friend, Tiffany Frank, also 21. They were riding in Mohr's 1992 Isuzu Rodeo.[6]

According to published reports, Mohr came up behind a 1994 Dodge Colt driven by 27 year-old Kraal Wiggins. They got into an altercation and Mohr eventually passed Wiggins' Colt.

After Wiggins pulled in behind Mohr's Rodeo, which was now in the center lane, Mohr slammed on his brakes. Wiggins couldn't stop his colt in time and slammed into the rear of the Rodeo.

Mohr lost control of his Rodeo, which rolled over and threw Tiffany Frank from the vehicle. She suffered multiple fractures and was airlifted to a local hospital and listed in fair condition. Neither Tiffany Frank nor Mohr had seat belts on at the time of the rollover.

Mohr was arrested and charged with aggravated vehicular assault.

It is unknown whether Tiffany decided to find a new boyfriend or not.

Chapter Four

Forcing Others Off the Road
And Vehicle Ramming

Twenty-Three Seniors Die in Louisiana
Bus Crash

Just before 9:00 am on Mother's Day, May 9, 1999, a seniors casino club was heading eastbound on Highway 610 near La Place, Louisiana. They had boarded the charter bus for a day trip to Casino Magic, a favorite casino in Bay St. Louis on Mississippi's gulf coast.[7]

Witnesses said a white car cut sharply in front of the bus, causing it to change lanes, then cut it off a second time, causing it to leave the roadway and crash into an embankment.

A woman said she saw people flying out of the bus windows. Some were in their 80's.

Of the 46 seniors aboard the bus, 23 lay dead. All due to a driver's indifference to their safety and right to life.

At the time of this writing, the driver of the white car has not yet been found.

Drivers Ed Teacher Resigns after Instructing Student to Give Chase

On September 19, 1997, in Durham, North Carolina, high school drivers education teacher David Cline had two female students with him in a drivers education vehicle as he set out to teach them the rules of the road. [8]

One of the girls was at the wheel. They had traveled about 20 miles from the school and were near Chapel Hill when they were cut off by another driver.

Instantly angered, Cline instructed the student driver to pursue the other car. They chased the other driver, 23-year-old Jon David Macklin, a waiter, until he stopped.

Reportedly, Cline then punched Macklin in the nose, causing it to bleed. Macklin (understandably) took off again, at which Cline again instructed the girl to chase him down a second time.

Thankfully, however, they could not catch up to him again. Police pulled Cline and his two students over for speeding. Cline was arrested and later released on $400 bail. The girl was reportedly not ticketed.

Toyota Takes On Semi: Toyota Loses

How many people would try something like this?

On Sunday, Oct. 10, 1999, on Interstate 40 near the Big I Interchange in Albuquerque, New Mexico, the driver of a black Toyota sedan reportedly got upset with a truck driver.

According to published reports, 53-year-old Abdul Sukhyani became upset when he felt a semi-truck had pulled too closely in front of him. He pulled up next to the truck and started honking his horn and tried to pull sharply in front of the truck.[9]

However, the little Toyota clipped the front of the semi and spun out of control, striking another car. The accident closed the highway for two hours.

Incredibly, the only injury was to Sukhyani's wife, Mountez Sukhyani, who suffered an injured jaw.

At this writing, the legal outcome of this incident is not known. However, just the fact that someone would take on an 80,000 lb. semi-tractor-trailer rig with a 2,000 lb. Toyota is enough to make one pause and think!

Vehicle Rammings

In Pursuit of Justice

On August 15, 1999, an 18-year-old was arrested in Akron, Ohio, for allegedly ramming another vehicle. The driver claimed that the other driver had struck and hit his father, a pedestrian, and that is why he pursued and rammed the other vehicle.[10]

A Broken Back

On Interstate 94 just south of Racine, Wisconsin, Mark Weckesser and Kenny Kelsey became angry with one another and began exchanging obscene gestures as they sped down the highway. The two drivers had apparently both been trying to get into the same lane, and neither was willing to yield.

Eventually, Weckesser maneuvered his car behind Kelsey and rammed him, sending his pickup into a concrete highway divider. Kelsey's back was broken instantly.

Weckesser was later arrested and charged with a felony (endangering safety).

A Freeway Joust Ends in Death

In October 1998, Terence Salisbury and Brian Bowser became entwined in a mutual fit of road rage as they traveled on Interstate 275 near Detroit.[11]

After they had jousted for some distance, Salisbury's vehicle was struck, and he lost control, smashing into an oncoming truck. Salisbury was killed.

Bowser pleaded no contest to the felony.

Family of Four is Forced Off the Road

On August 25, 1999, Denise Koenigs of Hales Corners, Wisconsin, was allegedly forced off the road as she and her family drove along Highway 60 near Pike Lake.[12]

She said she had slowed down to let the car behind her pass when that driver, Jerald Van Lear, 53, apparently became upset and began to pass her on the passenger side.

He reportedly struck her car at least twice, then forced Mrs. Koenig's car to cross a median and two traffic lanes.

Mr. Van Lear was charged with four counts of recklessly endangering safety.

As of this writing, the case has not yet been settled.

You're Not Going to Pass Me! - Five Die

In September 1998, William Glerum pleaded guilty and was sentenced to six months in jail for causing the deaths of five people, three of them children. The accident happened in upstate New York.[13]

Earlier that year, on April 26, Mr. Glerum had reportedly sped up and refused to allow another car to pass him, causing the accident. The car that couldn't pass veered into oncoming traffic and struck a third car, causing the fatalities.

Police said that Glerum and the driver of the other car had had an angry verbal exchange in traffic just prior to the accident.

Chapter Five

Roadside Stabbings, Beatings, Assaults

In April of 1997, 19-year-old Buffy Marie Hogg of Edmonds, Washington, attended a movie in nearby Lynnwood. Also in the theater, and sitting close by, was a 16-year-old.[14]

According to police reports, Hogg became upset at the 16-year-old for laughing too loudly during the movie. Later, she apparently approached the younger girl and stabbed her. Although this incident had nothing to do with road rage, it does serve to illustrate just how violent our society has become. Sometimes, such vicious attacks can erupt on our roads as well.

In this chapter, we compile a series of true life attacks which have occurred on the roadways of the world. Some resulted in injuries or death, others not, but they all have one thing in common: angry people behaving badly. And in some cases, displaying dangerous, even deadly acts of anger.

Like it or not, lower statistics or not, few can deny that we live in a very violent world these days. Incidents like the movie stabbing described above are all too common nowadays.

You can get into a lot of trouble fast for doing little or next to nothing. All you have to do is be in the wrong place at the wrong time and commit a driving error. And just in case you might be thinking that being an older person might help protect you from attack, think again. There is little pity for older people among many of our youth. Likewise, if you think an older person is less capable of inflicting a fatal attack on you for a minor clash, look out. You might just find yourself under attack by someone's grandpa.

Stoplight Stabbing - An Old Vigilante Attacks with a Knife

Lansing Michigan

When most of us think of a 67-year-old man, we think, "Mellow. Grandfatherly. Silver-haired, wise old gentleman." However, it seems these days that age is no guarantor of wisdom. On the contrary, it's possible that many older folks these days, just like some of their younger fellow drivers, are beginning to crack behind the wheel and lose all control.

So you don't think an older person can't lose his cool and attack you with a deadly weapon? Think again...

Get out of My Way!

Sixty-seven-year-old David Purnell didn't like the way Robert Boshea, 31, was driving. According to news accounts, Boshea had been driving his van in front of Purnell, who was driving his Cadillac, in a 35 mph zone on Miller Road in Lansing, Michigan.[15]

Angered by Boshea's slow moving van, Purnell allegedly drove around and got in front of him just before the next light. When the light turned green, Purnell refused to move.

Only seconds before the light turned red, Purnell sped through the intersection. Boshea followed.

At the next light, the two men got out of their vehicles, and Purnell stabbed Boshea in the chest. A Lansing police cadet reportedly witnessed the attack. Luckily, Boshea was treated at a nearby hospital and released. Purnell was charged with intent to murder, which is a felony and carries a sentence of life in prison.

Older Driver Beaten Unconscious

James McAmis, 60, of Eastpointe, Michigan, was allegedly beaten unconscious by a 32-year-old driver.[16]

The suspect apparently became enraged after McAmis ran a stoplight in his van and the suspect's 38-year-old girlfriend was injured. The suspect and his girlfriend were in a Jeep.

Enraged, the suspect grabbed a metal pipe and smashed the windows on McAmis's van. He then dragged the 60-year-old out of the van and began beating him. Witnesses apparently grabbed the suspect and held him down until police arrived as McAmis lay unconscious.

McAmis and the suspect's girlfriend were taken to a local hospital and both listed in serious condition.

Police said the suspect was not at fault in the accident, but due to his subsequent actions, he was arrested and now faces criminal charges for the beating.

Scholarly Lesson:
The Professor and the DEA Agent

The following event is an example of two drivers, both of whom are professional people, who completely lost their cool.

On a Friday evening on Wisconsin Interstate 43, a college assistant professor allegedly cut off another driver, a Drug Enforcement Administration agent. According to published police accounts, the agent said the fact that the professor cut him off caused him to lose his cool. The agent switched on his high beams and began to follow the professor.[17]

The two men eventually stopped on a city street in Madison and began to argue. A crowd soon gathered and stood in amazement as the two men went at each other.

The agent said he had observed the professor driving his gray Saab "recklessly, almost forcing vehicles off the freeway," and decided to follow him.

After both of them pulled off the highway, the agent saw the professor park in front of a residence. The agent pulled his pickup truck in behind the professor's car.

Reportedly, the professor got out of his car and charged screaming and swearing back to the agent's truck and grabbed him as he opened his truck door.

As the professor was yelling at the agent, he apparently reached into his pants pocket and pulled-out a loaded Colt semi-automatic handgun, the report said.

The police report stated that the agent then punched the professor in the chest, causing him to drop the gun back into his pocket. *(At one point, they reportedly both asked a passing cab driver to call the police).*

The report then said that the agent pulled out his service revolver and attempted to take the professor into custody. Another passing cab driver stopped and assisted the agent in detaining the professor until uniformed officers arrived.

At the time of this writing, the professor has not been identified, since he has not been charged. He disputed the police report, calling it "completely wrong and inaccurate."

One thing is for sure, both of these men were very lucky to escape with only minor injuries. Few fights between two people, both with guns, end without a shot being fired in anger.

The towns and hamlets of the South and Midwest are far from Los Angeles and New York. These are places not normally thought of as serious road rage candidates. However, towns all across the U.S., whether large, small, or tiny, are experiencing plenty of rudeness and violence in their communities and on their roads:

Reportedly, the professor got out of his car and charged screaming and swearing back to the agent's truck and grabbed him as he opened his truck door.

Roadside Stabbings

During the last week of July 1997, a 22-year-old man was stabbed to death in Milwaukee by another motorist. Apparently, the attacker had become angry when the car the victim had been riding in passed in front of him.

In Lansing Michigan, a 31-year old man was stabbed for "driving too slow."

Mike Tyson Attacks Two Motorists in a Minor Fender Bender

Consider the plight of two unfortunate motorists who had a minor fender bender with world champion boxer, Mike Tyson. Talk about fearing for your life, *not to mention your ears.*

On February 6, 1999, Tyson was sentenced to two years in jail for the August 31, 1998, attack in Gaithersburg, Maryland.[18]

Tyson apparently lost his cool after his Mercedes, which his wife was driving, was "bumped" from behind by Richard Hardick's car at a stoplight. Hardick's car was subsequently struck from behind by another car, driven by Abmielec Saucedo.

Tyson reportedly got out of his Mercedes and confronted the two men. He then punched Saucedo, 62, in the face and kicked 50-year-old Hardick in the groin, injuring both men.

In his decision, Judge Stephen Johnson stated that he was troubled that Tyson had attacked "not young, strong, or vigorous people." The two men filed civil suits, but they were settled out of court.

Tyson also paid a paltry $5,000 fine and had to perform 200 hours of community service. (Maybe he will give a few lectures on the perils of being a bad guy. I can hear it now: "My fellow man, *lend me your ear...*")

Cab Driver Kicks Pregnant Woman

On September 26, 1999, a 28-year-old pregnant woman and two of her friends went shopping in Akron, Ohio. On the return trip home, they took a cab driven by 47-year-old Brett Marston.[19]

According to reports, the three women took some time in coming up with the $5.75 cab fare between them, causing Marston to become upset.

When the victim demanded her correct change, Marston allegedly refused. She kept insisting, until he kicked her. She was sent to a local hospital, suffering vaginal bleeding.

Marston was charged with second degree recklessly endangering safety. (Nice guy, aye?)

The Knife and Pit Bull Brawl

On Thursday, September 23, 1999, a mass fight broke out on Madison, Wisconsin's east side as a result of an earlier road rage altercation.[20]

Kristine Broske, 17, told police that she had been picked up by Emmanuel Ocasio and Jessie Ditsch and that they were later tailgated by a green sport utility vehicle. She said the vehicle had followed them to Sprang and Hoard streets, near Oscasio's home, where a fight ensued.

Broske stated that she had run into the house to get a pit bull terrier for protection. However, the dog apparently got loose and charged into the brawl. Another of the brawlers ran into the house and brought out a knife.

Police later found out that Ocasio had seven outstanding warrants for his arrest.

Man's Face Slashed with Garden Shears

On June 9, 1998, two male drivers exited their vehicles near an intersection in Pacific Beach, California, and began to fight.[21]

One of the men had apparently stopped his van suddenly at the intersection, causing the driver behind him to honk his horn. The driver of the van subsequently flipped the other driver the finger.

According to police reports, the fight became more serious when one of the men, Pedro Naranjo, reportedly produced a pair of garden shears and slashed the other man's face.

Elderly Man Attacked and Killed

A tragedy occurred in Jacksonville, Florida, just two weeks prior to the Timmy Scully road rage murder, which also occurred in Jacksonville, and is described in the next chapter. David Sembach, Sr., was 78 years old at the time of his death. He was also the father of an assistant chief sheriff in the Jacksonville Sheriff's office.[22]

According to police records, Mr. Sembach made a driving error. He nearly hit Max Michael Pruett, 23, and Daniel Wesley Butler, 19, as they crossed Tiffany Road at an intersection. Pruett and Butler subsequently attacked David Sembach. In the scuffle that ensued, Sembach broke his hip. Two days later, he died of a blood clot caused by the fracture.

Getting off Easy

You might think in such a brutal case, that justice would prevail and Pruett and Davis, obviously dangerous fellows, would be locked up for some length of time.

However, on October 16, 1997, Daniel Wesley Butler, plead guilty to aggravated assault (he was found not guilty of murder) and sentenced to 1 year in jail and a $253 traffic fine.

On February 20, 1998, Pruett was found guilty of aggravated assault. He was sentenced to five years in prison and ordered to take "anger control" classes and serve 200 hours of community service. He was also ordered to apologize to the family of the victim.

Teen is Killed in Road Attack

On May 25, 1998, two 18-year-olds and 15-year-old Marco Rubalcalvas were chased down a street in Glendale, Arizona, after an argument. Police said the combatants traveled at speeds up to 90 mph.[23]

Marco and his companions were eventually caught and brutally beaten by their attackers. Marco died of massive head injuries the same day.

The case is still open.

Woman Jumps from Bridge after Being Beaten in Road Rage Attack

In August, 1995, a particularly brutal example of road rage occurred in Detroit, Michigan.[24]

Martell Welch, Jr., a large man at 6-foot-1, became enraged when he was bumped from behind twice by another driver, Deletha Word. They were on a crowded bridge.

According to reports, Welch exited his vehicle and drug the 115-pound Word from her car, beat her up and tore her clothes.

When he approached her again in his rage, she leaped off the bridge. She fell to her death some 30 feet below.

Welch was later convicted of second degree murder.

Chapter Six

Shootings on the Highway

The crime of murder, although reportedly on the decline in many areas, appears to be increasing on our nation's highways. Are these murderous attacks on drivers isolated to cities like Los Angeles or New York? No, not by any means. Spontaneous, rage filled attacks are occurring not only in our larger cities, but also in medium and small towns across the U.S. To gain a better understanding of this growing trend, let's take a look at a few road rage shooting cases that have occurred in small-to-average sized U.S. towns.

Brookfield, Wisconsin: A man was accused of pointing a gun at another driver after a February 7, 1998, argument on Calhoun Road. Authorities said the man had forced the other driver into oncoming traffic when Andrews cut him off.

As of this writing, the perpetrator has pleaded not guilty. According to a criminal complaint, the man with the gun told police that he displayed the weapon to the other driver, who had cursed at him, to end the dispute because he has a nervous condition that requires medication. Unfortunately, not all gun-related incidents end without a shot being fired...

Timmy Scully is Gunned Down

Jacksonville Florida: On June 5, 1997, 37-year old Timmy Scully of Jacksonville, Florida, was driving along on Washington Street minding his own business. Little did he know the danger that lay ahead. He would never reach his destination that day.[25]

Approaching from the opposite direction, was 56-year old Joseph Burl Walters. Both men were driving pickup trucks.

In an odd close call, the side view mirrors on their trucks hit as they passed each other. According to police accounts, Joseph Walters became enraged and shot Timmy Scully to death in the roadway.

On March 11, 1998, Joseph Burl Walters was found guilty and sentenced to 25 years in prison.

Although justice appears to have been served in this case, Catherine Scully, Timmy's wife of 19 years, must now live the rest of her life without him. How can there be justice?

Reader beware!! Drivers like Joseph Burl Walters are out there...maybe in the next pickup truck you meet.

Laura MacPhee Is Shot and Killed

A traffic encounter. A gesture. Laura MacPhee is killed. Like Jennifer Hywari, Laura MacPhee was 22 years old when she was killed on Interstate 94 in Minneapolis-St. Paul. But unlike Jennifer's case, where a vehicle was used as a weapon, Laura was shot to death by three mean youths just out looking for trouble.[26]

Laura and Laurens Matton, 22, had been friends since childhood. They had gone to their high school prom together. They liked to spend time together going to bars, seeing friends, and just generally having a good time. They treasured each other's friendship. Laura had grown up living in both Minneapolis and St. Paul, alternating time with both her parents, who are divorced. Laurens and Laura had remained friends since childhood and had dated on and off.

A Morning Drive Across Town

On Friday morning, as Laura and Laurens drove along on East Seventh Street, the assailants pulled in front of the pair and gestured at them. Matton, who was at the wheel, raised his hands and gestured with his shoulders in a "what gives" manner. The assailants then followed them onto I-94, where a shot was fired near the Dale Street exit. Laura was struck in the head and killed.

About an hour later, three youths were picked up by police while trying to steal a car. One was 17 years old, the other two were 16. Their descriptions matched those of the suspects involved in the shooting. Their names were withheld due to their ages.

Reports made to police prior to the shooting indicate that the suspects may have been harassing other motorists before Laura was killed. The youths had stolen the car they were riding in.

The next day, as he was interviewed by reporters, Patrick MacPhee, Laura's father, sat thumbing through old photographs of his slain daughter, remembering the times he had spent with her. He referred to Laura as his "best buddy." Mr. MacPhee also has two sons who were 11 and 13 at the time of the shooting.

"It's tearing my heart and my gut up," he said. "I've seen a lot of gunfire. I've dealt with a lot of death out there in Vietnam. I wasn't prepared for this," he continued.

Mouthed Words and Smiles

Laurens Matton later gave the police a detailed account of what had happened during the deadly encounter.

Apparently, Matton had passed the three suspects in the stolen white Toyota sedan at a light. The Toyota then veered into Matton's lane in front of him. At the next light, Matton saw the suspects mouthing words at him. Matton then mouthed words back to the youths, and smiled at them. They smiled back. Later, Matton noticed the car following them as he entered the freeway. The shooting occurred moments later.

Matton later recalled to reporters about what he saw in the youths' faces that morning: "It was just evil, up to no good," Matton said, as he described the look in their eyes. "[Like] they'd lost something. All they could think about was evilness."

"I wanted to run them off the road, but does a negative and a negative make a positive?" he said. "Some people hold grudges forever. I just hope some day they relive this and they rethink it, and it might totally change them."

Just Getting Started in Life

Laura's family said that she was excited about starting out on her own. A new time in her life. At the bar the night before her death, she talked excitedly to friends about finally moving out on her own with a friend. She had lived with her father in Minneapolis for about three years. Laura dated often and enjoyed the single life. Her office job in Edina was earning her enough money to leave home and start a life of her own. She also loved to spend time with her friends. Her father, Patrick, had been planning to buy her a TV for her new place. Now, one day after her death, he said that he might have to sell her car to pay for her funeral.

"I loved her with all my heart," Mr. MacPhee said. "She could walk into a room with her smile and you couldn't resist her."

A Father's Road Rage Kills His Own Son

It was Saturday morning, April 17, 1999. William J. Morrison 50, and his three children, including his son, 17-year-old Jamie, were southbound in their pickup truck on Lake Pleasant Road in the town of Peoria, a suburb of Phoenix, Arizona. William Morrison was behind the wheel.[27]

At some point, Morrison became enraged after an altercation with a man driving a smaller pickup, 23-year-old Luis Salas of Laveen, Arizona. According to APB 911 News, the situation rapidly heated up, and both drivers pulled to the side of the road and stopped.

Once stopped, both Morrison and Salas exited their vehicles and a struggle began. Shortly after, Jamie Morrison was shot and killed.

At the time this story broke, Salas who had fired the shot, had not been charged. Jamie's father, however, had been charged with causing the death of his own son.

According to Peoria Police Sgt. Shawn Gormley, some people find it difficult to comprehend how a man can shoot another and yet not be charged with a crime. "If you're in a position where you are forced to defend your life, you're allowed to use deadly physical force," Gormley said. Reportedly, the gun that killed Jamie belonged to William Morrison. Under Arizona's felony-murder law, anyone committing a crime is responsible for any deaths which result from committing that crime.

"Basically," Gormley continued, "had [Morrison] not done what he did ... a series of things throughout the event ... his son would not have died."

Salas Felt Trapped

Sgt. Gormley went on to describe how Salas had been "painted into a corner." Reportedly, he, too, had two passengers, including a baby, in his truck. The baby slept through the shooting.

Salas fled the scene and was found later that same evening in Laveen, which is 30 miles from the scene of the shooting. Police said Salas also suffered injuries from the incident, but didn't elaborate.

Chapter Seven

Big-Rig Rage:
Attacked by an Eighteen Wheeler

There is nothing on our highways that is larger, heavier, or potentially more deadly than a fully loaded tractor-trailer rig in the wrong hands. Truck drivers are considered worldwide to be some of the most expert drivers anywhere. However, when there is a mishap, or a driver "snaps" for some reason and goes after a smaller vehicle, the chances of survival for the smaller vehicle's passengers are low.

Because they weigh 80,000 pounds or more, a typical 3,000-pound car doesn't stand a chance against these highway behemoths. Few things could be more terrifying for a motorist than being run into, much less attacked and run over by, a semi-truck piloted by a madman. Such tales are fodder for Hollywood horror flicks. In real life, these things just don't happen. Or do they? Three teenagers, residents of the small town of Miami, Oklahoma, lived just such a terrifying moment. Amazingly, they somehow survived. Here's their story.

Three Teens are Run Over by Semi-Tractor Trailer

A preliminary telephone discussion with 13th Judicial District Attorney, Ben Loring, and Assistant District Attorney, Bill Culver, both of Miami, convinced me to make a trip to the small Oklahoma town. There seemed to be a lot to learn about this horrendous case of road rage.

"Before I became a lawyer, I was a cop for 21 years," said Culver. "I got to the scene very quickly, and I just knew we had dead people. To this day, I still cannot believe anyone could live through that. That little truck was completely demolished." He continued, "There was an angel in that truck with those boys. They missed death only by inches."

As I sat listening to Mr. Culver's recollection of the attack and the trial just ended, I sorted through numerous photos of the scene. They were shot from various angles, and I too, could not believe that anyone could still be alive in the little truck, which had been severely crushed.

It was also hard to believe that anyone would deliberately try to kill another human being, especially a stranger, in such a brutal manner and after such little provocation. How could a simple traffic infraction cause someone to commit attempted murder? Let's take a look at what unfolded that day.

Three Boys Just Going to School

Ronald Abernathy, 18, and his two school buddies: Richie Powers, 18, and Michael Davis, 17, were enjoying an average Oklahoma spring day.

They were traveling old Route 66 in Abernathy's small 1988 Mazda extended-cab pickup truck. The trio were on their way to Picher-Cardin High School for afternoon classes, having just finished their usual morning classes at the Oklahoma Technical School, about five miles from Miami.

Ronald Abernathy was at the wheel while Richie Powers sat next to him. Michael Davis, who is hearing impaired, was stretched out sideways behind them, across the bench seat. (About the only way a long teenager can ride comfortably in such tight quarters).

An Enraged Truck Driver

Trifon Lee Athnos, 37, was low on cash. He had also been angry at his employer, May Trucking, of Salem, Oregon. Things just weren't going his way as of late.

A 14-year Marine Corps veteran, Athnos had been in Beirut when the barracks was bombed. He was proud of his military service, but now, he was fighting a different kind of battle. He was in the grips of financial disaster. So bad was his predicament, that he had exited Highway 44 at the Missouri-Oklahoma border to avoid paying the Oklahoma Turnpike fee. He just didn't have the money to pay the toll. Now, mile after mile of two-lane roads through small towns, traffic lights, and slow traffic lay ahead of him. He was not a happy man.

Ron, Rich, and Mike, were typical 90's teens. They were fun loving and maybe just a little arrogant. But as we all know, youth matures into adulthood soon enough. Like all teens, they just liked to have fun. And, like most teenage boys, they didn't like getting pushed around. They would stand up for themselves when challenged.

However, their first mistake that day was trying to pass the wrong truck driver. As the teens came up behind Athnos's truck in a construction zone, Ron noticed that the truck was moving extremely slow. Police records showed that Athnos was traveling between 15 and 20 miles an hour in a 40 mph zone. Although construction zones are "no-passing" zones and Abernathy was technically in the wrong to pass the truck, the boys were in a hurry to get to school, and the truck was traveling at a ridiculously slow speed.

After making sure the road ahead was clear, Abernathy steered his Mazda pickup into the oncoming lane and began to pass the crawling tractor- trailer rig.

However, just as the pickup started to pass, Athnos whipped his truck over into the left lane, nearly striking the little pickup. Abernathy swerved, slammed on his brakes, and backed off. In the next instant, Athnos gave the boys the finger, and they, according to court statements, returned the gesture in kind. The trio was in disbelief as to what had just happened. Was this guy crazy? Why would he deliberately try to run them off the road, or worse, run them over?

A Short Cut

Next, the now angry teens, knowing the back streets of Miami well, took a short cut through town in an effort to get ahead of the trucker. They knew he would have to continue through town on the truck route, so they drove several blocks ahead and waited for him at the intersection of North Main Street and 22nd Avenue.

According to police reports, the teens wanted to confront Athnos and ask him "what his problem was." Displaying youthful over-exuberance, they wanted to "read him the riot act" for what he had done.

When Athnos approached the intersection, the teens began yelling at him to get out, at which Athnos yelled back and again gave them the finger. The trio promptly returned the gesture and four letter words, as Athnos drove on. Aggravated, but finally sensing that this was one crazy truck driver, the teens decided that it might be time to leave him alone and get to school. But it was too late. They had already lit this driver's short fuse.

The teens drove down another set of back streets, emerging back onto the main drag at a stoplight. There were two cars in front of them as they came to a stop and sat waiting for the light to turn green.

Athnos's Semi and the Pickup after the Assault

Suddenly, within about five to ten seconds of sitting at the light, Abernathy saw Athnos's semi in his rear-view mirror coming at them from behind. He only had enough time to exclaim "Oh Sh........"

Real-Life Horror Flick

As in a real-life Hollywood horror film, Athnos, upon seeing the youths directly in front of him, had instantly snapped and floored his powerful rig.

Eye witnesses who were at the intersection said they heard the semi's engine revving up. They also saw black smoke pouring from the exhaust stack as Athnos set his sights on the three youths and powered his rig toward them.

Only a second or two before the impact, Abernathy turned his pickup to the right and hit the gas pedal in an attempt to get away through a parking lot. Now, he was standing on the brakes with all he had in him. But, despite his efforts, the huge rig was pushing the little truck forward and simultaneously coming up over the top of the truck bed, crushing it as it came. In mere seconds, without a miracle, the cab would be crushed as well with the teens inside.

Staring Death in the Face

Michael Davis, who was lying prone across the back seat, later gave dramatic testimony to investigators, saying that he had read Athnos's lips as he looked up at the raging driver. *Since he was hearing impaired, his aunt signed for him at the trial as he recounted his side of the story to investigators.*

Davis said that Athnos said, "I'm trying to kill you!" as he looked down on the terrified, helplessly trapped young man.

A Life-Saving Miracle

According to police records and backed up by the photos taken at the accident scene, the only thing that saved the teens lives was a metal telephone pole. As Athnos slammed his semi into the little truck and pushed it forward, simultaneously riding up and over it, the left front of the pickup hit the metal pole. This caused the pickup to spin ninety degrees to the left. This turning action took most of the cab just out from under the semi as it continued forward over the top of the bed.

(When it was all over, the rear half of the pickup truck was only about 18 inches thick under the crushing weight of the semi).

The telephone pole that spun the pickup truck to the left, barely saving the boys lives, can be seen in the left of this photo.

"Get Away from Michael!"

Ron Abernathy and Richie Powers, though bruised with minor cuts, and partially in shock, somehow crawled out of the mangled wreckage on their own. When they looked up, they were terrified to see Athnos reaching into the back seat of their truck, where their friend Michael Davis lay pinned and bleeding.

According to court documents, Athnos had used his belt as a tourniquet to try to control the serious bleeding from one of Michael's arms. *Apparently, his Marine Corps first-aid training told him that he had to stop the bleeding fast, or the boy could die.*

"Get away from Mike, you son of a.....!," one of the teens yelled. The two banged-up teens, not knowing what Athnos was doing to Michael, instantly tried to pick a fight with the ex-Marine. However, luckily, a bystander got between Athnos and the two boys. *(Even an out of shape 37-year-old ex-Marine is capable of lethal combat, especially against an untrained opponent).*

Understandably, though, in their shock and anguish, the boys just didn't know if Athnos, who had tried to kill them just moments before, was trying to hurt Michael or help him. Their first reaction was to try to defend their helplessly trapped buddy.

It took firefighters 20 minutes to free Michael from the wreckage. Although one of his arms was severely injured and he had numerous cuts and abrasions, he survived his injuries. It was also incredible that there was no fire, since diesel fuel had spilled everywhere, and the little pickup truck had been smashed nearly flat. It's also amazing that the pickup's gas tank didn't rupture. If there had been a fire, all three boys might have been burned alive. Certainly,

Michael Davis, trapped in the tangled wreckage, would have perished.

Attempted Murder
"Athnos...Take Me to Jail"

Miami Police Officer Tony McCoy was the first officer at the scene. According to police testimony, as Officer McCoy approached Athnos, he said, "You may just as well take me to jail...I ran over them on purpose." Apparently, another officer and two of the teens also heard him confess.

Officer McCoy's first concern was Michael, still trapped in the back seat, so he sat Athnos down and told him to stay put. Later, Athnos was charged with three counts of "using deadly force to attempt killing another," which is equivalent to attempted murder. His bond was set at $300,000.

These teenagers are three very lucky young men. Miraculously, they had survived. They will forever remember this potentially deadly semi-tractor-trailer rig attack. An enraged truck driver and his heavy load are not something to mess with on the highway or in town. It is also important to remember that these three teens were not completely innocent, at least in terms of social behavior. They cussed back at the driver, they returned the middle finger, and they taunted this already disturbed man into lethal retribution. They broke what behavioral experts call the "social rules of the road," or in better terms, the "highway survival rules."

Athnos Pleads "No Contest"

Prior to Athno's trial date, no fewer than 13 eyewitnesses were prepared to testify against him. There were witnesses to the first encounter, when Athnos tried to swerve into the teens, the second encounter, and the vehicular assault itself.

One witness saw Athnos very angry several blocks before the assault. This same witness saw black smoke coming from the exhaust stack and no brake lights on the semi as it smashed into the pickup.

According to prosecution records, Athnos' ex-wife stated that he had abused pills in the past. (Although there was no evidence of alcohol or drug abuse in this case.) He had also been abusive to their eldest son. Apparently, according to his ex-wife, Athnos had quite a history of being hot tempered and was quick to lose his cool.

On April 7, 1998, just six days prior to his trial for assault and attempted murder, Athnos, aware of the mountain of evidence against him, pleaded "no contest" to all charges. District Judge Sam C. Fullerton sentenced him to 11 years in prison on each count, to run concurrently. He was also fined $3,000 and ordered to pay restitution to the boys' families (including medical expenses and the value of the pickup not covered by insurance).

Prelude to Disaster

Today, many semi-tractors have computers mounted in the cab close to the driver. With these computers, drivers and their dispatchers can send and receive messages back and forth via a satellite link. A driver based in California, for example, can communicate with his dispatcher while traveling across Florida, Maine, or Quebec. Trifon Lee Athnos had just such a computer on board his truck. This computer sent and received what are called, "Qualcomm Messages."

During the accident investigation (assault is more accurate), investigators searched Athnos's truck cab and seized anything that could be used as evidence in the case. Some of the most interesting, and as it turned out, damaging pieces of evidence found and prepared for the trial, were the Qualcomm Messages in the semi's onboard computer.

Lighting the Fuse of Rage

Below is a transcript of the actual messages that Athnos sent and received. The messages begin on March 29, 1997, just six days before he snapped and ran over the three teenagers. As these computer log messages demonstrate, Athnos was having severe financial and emotional problems. This once proud Marine had had to borrow "survival money" from his father. He had pleaded repeatedly for financial help from his trucking firm, complaining bitterly about having to use his own money to support their operation. According to Athnos's messages, they had not been paying him (although it also appears that some of the blame may have rested on Athnos himself for not turning in receipts on time. In fact, he may have owed the trucking company money).

Whatever the reasons, because of his sporadic pay, he had been unable to pay his child support. His truck had also broken down for 13 days, which helped fuel his anger and financial despair. Athnos was down and out, and in his mind, he was already driving down "Skid Row."

The most obvious story that unfolds in these transcripts, which prosecutors skillfully used to prepare for the trial, was his increasing, ever-building anger, which grew over the days just prior to the assault.

Unknowingly, the three young men were about to taunt a man who was facing bankruptcy and financial ruin, sitting on top of 300 horse power and some 40 tons of crushing weight. Trifon Lee Athnos had just gone off the deep end. He was broke and desperate.

As you can see in the transcript, in the hours just before he encountered the young men, a deep, explosive rage had been building inside Athnos. *All that was needed was a finger to pull his hair trigger temper. In the case of the three teens, that finger would be the middle one.....in triplicate.*

March 29, 1997...."Qualcomm Messages"

15:06 Hours
Athnos to Dispatcher: "Truck problems fixed....is it legal to run if the left hand trailer-side turn signal is missing?"

Reply from Dispatcher: "Yes...."

The following message is also from the dispatcher, and is in response to Athnos on an earlier question he had about "lumping." Lumping refers to having to pay someone to unload the cargo of the truck because the dock refuses to, or delays him for hours. This costs the driver time and money. Lumping is a major headache for truck drivers.

Dispatcher: "To get paid for unloading, you must get written documentation on the bill or a receipt...."

19:02 Athnos: "Trailer lights out....looks like sabotage - all wires have been pulled - kept driving to nearest town...."

19:04 Athnos: "Pins not on wires - pulled-out...will try for Highway Patrol escort, next truck stop - Do not send wrecker - too much money - thanks."

19:14 Dispatcher: "What do you want me to do tonight?"

19:15 Athnos: "Discovered problem....never mind....got help....we will rebuild connector....we have the technology....sorry to bother you again....have a good Easter."

(Athnos had earlier asked for and was sent directions to Von Frozen Foods, in Santa Anna, Ontario, Canada, to drop off a delivery)

March 30, 1997

07:39 Athnos: "Consignor not receiving [loads] till 10:00....no outside lumpers [no dock help that he can hire to unload his truck]...I have no medical insurance....I just got over pneumonia two weeks ago...."

07:48   Athnos: "Required $140 for lumper services....dock time limit equals 1,000 cases per hour, [which] equals 2.5 hours to unload....no can do by myself." [within the required time limit at the dock]. "Called Phil....he said that was SOP [standard operating procedure] here and he would authorize it....thx" [refers to reimbursement to Athnos for the money he spent paying the lumpers to unload his truck].

07:56   Athnos: "Also, please see if payroll will pay me for this load Friday....if so, what do they need from me?....I have no money for fax or anything.... I do have a bag of chips....I haven't cleared a paycheck now going on 7 weeks.... and tell Phil I have to send $100 a week for child support out of the money he has been sending me....thanks for your help...."

09:04   Athnos: "John (dispatcher), once you get my NT message, try like hell to get me a long haul (2,500 [miles] plus)....this way I can get out of the hole I'm in because of truck breakdowns....thx"

09:24   Athnos: "John, what is your fax number?....I will fax copies of all paperwork except VIR's, so you can give to payroll today so I can get paid for it....this week's trip to follow....thx."

11:42   Dispatcher: "Please turn in all supporting documentation for this trip as soon as possible at a local terminal....the paperwork for this trip must be received at the Brooks Terminal before you can get paid...."

March 31,1997 (traveling)

13:41   Athnos: "John, I just sent logs and bills fax....what is your last name?....and who is my payroll contact?....thx much...."

19:14 Athnos: "Please send $125 for pallets....I haven't got enough on me....F/M said OK for you to do it [to wire the money] so I can make the pickup....thx...."

20:35 Athnos: "I have perfectly good #2 pallets....shipper is telling me they wanted #1's....*I think they do this to sell pallets..*"

20:38 Dispatcher: "Where did you buy them and can you take them back so we can get #1's....?"

20:39 Athnos: "Shipper is only doing this to sell pallets at $9 each....you and I know this....if I'm to pay for it....no way....it is a ripoff...."

20:42 Athnos: "Called dispatcher - no answer....called Dad....he sent me enough so I can eat this week...."

20:44 Dispatcher: "So where are you going to get rid of the #2's....?"

20:46 Athnos: "Shipper is not going to get any more of my $ times 11 [pallets] then! x 11 ....nearest place is 50 miles away!....God, what next....?"

20:48 Dispatcher: "Are you still needing to get number 1 pallets?"

20:49 Athnos: "I don't know....let's get the pallets we need....I'll send CC...."

20:53 Athnos: "This means I've just lost a big chunk of change....I suppose [the] consignor will want unloading $$ too!....just bit my lip....no cussing allowed...."

21:11 Athnos: "I got thru Bakersfield on route....can turn #2's in AM....Shipper wants $158....will give credit for four of the #2's....need to change disposition info...."

21:20 Dispatcher: "OK, $158....will do so...." [sent check]

21:27 Athnos: *"Thanks, I came very close to losing it this time....you got me back into focus....it must be that darned comet I think...."*

21:29 Dispatcher: "Fly out of it....it may cause problems...."

23:27 Athnos: "Arrived ....[at] shipper"

April 1, 1997

23:27 Athnos: "Can you get a New Mexico permit faxed to pilot in Winslow?....I still haven't got my New Mexico cab card....my permit is two years old...."

23:29 Dispatcher: "We don't have the cab cards in this office....we will have to buy a permit...."

23:41 Athnos: "Caught in Flagstaff, Arizona.... blizzard...."

April 2, 1997

09:42 Dispatcher: "Call 1-888-806-xxxx about a car you have??....John."

09:43 Athnos: "I don't own a car...."

12:26 Athnos: "I would like to request the following days off....4/9 thru 4/12...."

12:38 Athnos: "Require reimbursement of $45 for New Mexico permit...."

14:41   Dispatcher: "Turn in receipt with paperwork and you will get reimbursed for the permit...."

16:44   Athnos: "John, can you find out if I will be getting any $ in tomorrow's pay? If not, can you get an estimate on how much I am still owing? If I can't clear any $ by next Friday, I will have to declare bankruptcy....I have only cleared $300 since February and $900 since January....thx."

April 4, 1997

09:10   Athnos: "That's week #7....no pay. No, I can't borrow no more $ from Phil or parents....that's it. Once I sell the pallets, I'll have enough to make one or two more runs....if no pay next week, I have no choice but bankruptcy...."

10:00   Dispatcher: "I would like to talk to you a little later about your no pay....this is Tena....send me a message later and I will get a number for you to call me...."

10:31   Athnos: (Last message he sent) *"Tena, I'll be going underground today in a cave....so I won't be able to contact you for awhile....nothing can be done about my pay problems, either....I clear something next week, or I'm done....13 days broke down....late trip packs....and a lot of slow freight...."*

10:40   Dispatcher: "Boy, I heard that....if you can handle it, the freight is picking up....we'll talk...."

Just over an hour later, at approximately 12:00 noon, Athnos ran over the three teenagers with his cheese-laden semi.

The last message investigators found on the damaged truck's onboard computer, came from the dispatcher to the truck the next morning, April 5, 1997, as it sat impounded as evidence. The trucking firm was apparently still unaware of what had happened:

0828: Dispatcher: "No arrival call yet......."

Lessons Learned

There is much to be learned from this case. First, however, it is very important to make a point here: *Trifon Lee Athnos is not typical of long-haul truck drivers.* As we will discuss in a later chapter, despite erroneous information to the contrary, truck drivers are, by accident statistics, the safest group of drivers on the roads today. Although there are "rogue truck drivers" out there, just as in other driver groups (and I have met a few), truck drivers are only about one-tenth as likely to be involved in an accident. More on this topic later......

Probably the most important thing to remember about this case is that when it comes to semi-tractor- trailer rigs and passenger vehicles, size and overall mass matters. You simply cannot win against a semi. So, even if you are completely in the right, get out of the way of that truck! Let the police handle the problem. You don't know that driver or his state of mind. Better to be right but wise and out of harm's way than to be "dead right." Don't tempt fate.

Last, but certainly not least, all of us drivers, regardless of our age or circumstances, are vulnerable at times. We don't know what that other guy or gal is going through out there on the road. There is too much anger on the highways of the world. Maybe you and I can do our small part by defusing ourselves and backing down whenever we are challenged. My guess is there are three teenage boys down in eastern Oklahoma who will from now on let sleeping dogs lie...

Semi-Tractor-Trailer Rig Runs Over Sleeping Camper

Shawn Neal Curran was a 34-year-old truck driver. He had lost his job as a trucker. He had just lost his girlfriend. He was on methamphetamines. Like Trifon Athnos, Shawn Curran had hit rock bottom. And soon, James Flannery, an innocent man would die.[28]

A Jealous Rage

In September, 1997, Curran went on trial for first-degree murder in a sad case of semi-tractor-trailer road rage.

This case demonstrates a temptation to retaliate with a big rig. A very small minority of truck drivers have occasionally been known to do such a terrible, deadly thing.

The same can be said for large vans and pickup trucks verses small subcompacts, for example. In every one of these cases, the brute power and massive weight of the larger vehicle is used by the attacker as an overpowering weapon against weaker metal, or as in this case, tent fabric and human flesh.

Campground Shoot-Out

Shawn Curran lived with his girlfriend in the Acorn Park Campground, which was conveniently located next door to his employer, where he was a truck driver. The campground is located on the Pala Indian Reservation, which is near Vista, California.

It was Friday morning, June 8, 1996. Curran had just been fired from his job that morning, less than 24 hours prior to the attack, for using methamphetamines. A band had been playing in the campground that Friday night, and two motorcycle clubs had gathered in the park to listen to the music, camp, and just have a good time. In all, some 300 campers were in the park.

Reportedly, Curran believed that his girlfriend had taken up with one of the band members, and that the bikers were "out to get him and his girlfriend," as Deputy District Attorney, Laura Rogers explained to me. "He said that he thought that he and his girlfriend were angels, and that the bikers were from Hell. He said he believed that they were going to kill both of them and bury them in the woods," she said.

Deputy DA Rogers, who prosecuted Curran, told the jury that Curran had "killing on his mind," when he fired up the Peterbilt after being fired from his job and headed for the campground *(apparently, he somehow still had the keys or an extra set)*.

According to the prosecution, Curran, in a fit of jealous rage, was searching for the musician whom he believed was having an affair with his girlfriend.

Curran entered the campground behind the wheel of the semi, sped through the park, and headed for the bandstand.

A number of the bikers opened fire on the truck's cab with their guns in an attempt to stop him.

Though his cab was riddled with bullets, Curran was unhurt. The semi hit two parked trucks and kept going. Immediately after hitting the parked trucks, the semi veered off the road, and a rear wheel on the trailer ran over James Flannery's head as he slept in his tent. His head was instantly "pulpified." He never knew what hit him. Mr. Flannery was 35 years old.

Also camped in the park that night, was a tent full of deaf people. An unidentified camper, at risk to his own life, pulled the deaf people out of the tent only seconds before Curran ran over it. "More bloodshed was narrowly avoided," Assistant DA Rogers said.

Curran managed to exit the park, but a sheriff's deputy found the truck stopped only a mile away, apparently out of fuel. (The tanks had been hit by the gunfire, too.) Curran fled on foot, only to be captured about five hours later at his mother's home.

Later, upon inspecting the truck, investigators found approximately 50 bullet holes in and around the cab. *The windshield alone had twelve slug holes in it, but amazingly, none of the shots had hit Curran.*

During the trial, prosecutors argued that Curran, although pleading insanity at the time of the attack due to hallucinations from the meth that he had been taking all day, still had enough presence of mind to locate the truck, start it up, and proceed toward the campground.

Shawn Curran was found guilty of second degree murder. Hopefully, he'll remain behind bars for a long time. And, hopefully, he'll never be behind the wheel of an 18-wheeler again.

Chapter Eight

Random Acts of Road Rage

Road Rage in Peoria

During the summer of 1997, a man driving a Mercedes was parked in front of a shoe shine shop on Adams Street, in Peoria, Illinois. After conducting his business, the driver pulled out in to the path of a man driving a Chevrolet Camaro. Although the cars didn't collide, the enraged Camaro driver jumped out of his car and began beating on the Mercedes.

By the time police arrived, the Camaro driver had done $1,500 damage to the Mercedes. If he had kept his cool, he would have driven away unscathed. Instead, his violent aggression caused him to be arrested for destruction of property. The Mercedes driver was cited for improper starting from a curve.

Both of these drivers were family men. The Mercedes driver was picking up his freshly shined shoes for his daughter's wedding the next day. The Camaro driver was taking his wife out to celebrate their wedding anniversary. Ordinary men, one of whom nearly caused an accident by carelessness, and the other exploding in a fit of small town road rage: fists against sheet metal.

Officer Assaulted by Tomato Throwing Produce Men

Milwaukee, Wisconsin, is generally considered a nice town, at least when compared with many other cities. However, aggressive driving and road rage can happen anytime, anywhere. Milwaukee is no exception.

Sgt. Mark Strachota of the Milwaukee Sheriff's Department is the leader the department's "Road Rage Squadron." As of this writing, this special squadron is only a few months old, but the results of their efforts are already evident. Unlike most states, where State Highway Patrols handle the duty, in Milwaukee, the Sheriff's Department patrols the highways in and around Milwaukee and its suburbs. Although like most law enforcement agencies, they do handle other law enforcement calls, their primary role is highway safety.[29]

"We have several deputies who are assigned to the special road rage patrol each day," said Sgt. Strachota. "Right now, we're using completely unmarked white Chevy Lumina's. The program has been very effective already."

"Our deputies drive along at about eight miles over the speed limit in traffic. We're not trying to encourage speeding, but we think anyone driving faster than eight miles over the posted limit is driving too fast. At this speed, we also have a pretty hard case if someone gets on the bumper of one of our cars and honks, screams, gestures, or in some other way becomes aggressive," Sgt. Strachota continued.

"In one recent incident, one of our deputies was on patrol when two men in a small produce truck became angry at him and cut him off, nearly pinning his car against a concrete wall. They were yelling obscenities at him as well.

"Then, the passenger in the truck threw a tomato at the officer's car. They sped away and exited the highway before the officer could recover and pursue the duo. It would not have been safe for the officer to cross several lanes of heavy traffic in pursuit.

"However, the deputy did have time to get the license number, and the name of the produce company was painted in large letters across the side of the truck. They were easy to find," said the Sergeant.

"At first, they denied being involved with any incident with a white Lumina. However, as the conversation progressed and the deputy told them it was he himself whom they had nearly pinned against the wall with their truck and thrown the retaliatory vegetable, they admitted the act."

According to Sgt. Strachota, two men learned a valuable lesson that day as they walked away with a pocket full of tickets.

According to Sgt. Strachota, the tomato thrower said, "If he had known that it was a deputy in the car, he would never have thrown the tomato."

In this author's opinion, what's the difference?

These two idiots not only stopped traffic by pinning the officer, a dangerous act in itself which could have caused an accident, but they used both their vehicle and a projectile, *albeit a tomato*, as a retaliatory weapon. What if a rock or baseball bat had been handy? A gun? Deputy or not, that officer is still a human being and they had no right stopping him or threatening him in any way.

Minivan –vs.- Suburban

On Thanksgiving Day, 1999, 46-year-old James Gearheart, driving his Suburban, suffered a broken left arm and leg and a concussion after a road rage incident on I-25 near Fort Collins, Colorado.[30]

According to police reports, Gearheart had been engaged in road rage with a minivan for some 20 miles at speeds up to 80 mph before he lost control and crossed the highway striking Robert Pulchipher, who was in a Mercedes SUV. Pulchipher was 63.

Pepper Mace and Ramming Kills Two

Although road rage has only recently been given much attention by the media, it isn't a new phenomenon. A particularly heinous event that illustrates this point happened back in 1994.

Just after 2:00 pm, on the afternoon of September 7, 1994, Illinois State Troopers were dispatched to a serious accident on Interstate 290 westbound, just east of Interstate 355, on Chicago's west side.[31]

According to witnesses cited in police reports, Albert Weems, 27, and Cozette Jones, 34, while riding in Weems's Blue Geo Tracker had been involved in a road rage attack. When troopers arrived, Jones lay dead along the side of the road and Weems was in serious condition with extensive lower body injuries.

Several witnesses stated that two men in a yellow Pontiac Firebird had struck the Tracker and run the two victims off the road after an ongoing road rage battle on the highway. They stated that they saw the two vehicles swerving in and out of traffic for some distance until they finally pulled over and two white or Hispanic men exited the Firebird, one holding what appeared to be bolt cutters.

One witness said he saw the man with the bolt cutters swinging them at the driver of the Tracker, then saw the Tracker pull back onto the highway to escape.

One of the witnesses then saw the Firebird try to sideswipe the Tracker several times as if to run it off the road. At one point, the driver of the Firebird reached out and began spraying a mist-like substance into the passenger side of the Tracker. The woman rolled up the window and leaned toward the driver to avoid the spray. (It later proved to be pepper spray.)

Moments later, the Tracker was hit from behind by the Firebird, made a 180 degree spin, hit a guardrail and rolled over, throwing Weems and Jones out of the vehicle.

Arthur G. Soleras was later stopped and charged with first-degree murder. Soleras was also charged with aggravated battery when it was discovered that he had sprayed capsium pepper spray into Weems's Tracker just prior to striking the vehicle with his Firebird.

Disabled Man and Son Beaten

In April, 1999, Bruce Brandenburger, 36, pleaded guilty to battery and substantial battery in Rock County, Wisconsin.[32]

According to published accounts, Brandenburger had been tailgating the 56-year-old victim, who had disabled license plates and walked with a cane, and his 23-year-old son.

At one point, Brandenburger apparently passed the victims in a no-passing zone, shaking his fist at them. The victim pulled over to avoid being hit, and Brandenburger also pulled over and approached the victim's vehicle.

He pulled the victim out of his car and began beating the disabled man in the face. When the victim's son tried to help his father, he was reportedly choked, punched in the face, and thrown down on the pavement.

The son suffered a cut face and three chipped teeth, and lost consciousness.

Brandenburger received 90 days in jail and four years probation.

The Crossbow Church Deacon

By now, most Americans have certainly heard about this now famous Massachusetts road rage attack. Here's a brief refresher.[33]

On February 20, 1994, 54-year-old Donald Graham, a church deacon and bookkeeper, became enraged during an on-going highway traffic dispute with Michael Blodgett, 42.

After several miles of antagonistic posturing on Interstate 95, both motorists pulled to the side of the road and exited their vehicles.

Soon after leaving his vehicle, Graham pulled a crossbow from his trunk and killed Blodgett with a 20-inch, razor sharp arrow.

Sara and Leo

On February 11, 2000, Sara McBurnett lost her little Bichon Frise dog, Leo, to an enraged driver after they had a minor fender bender. Sara was kind enough to allow me to interview her on May 4, 2000. This is Sara and Leo's story.

Sara had left her home in Lake Tahoe, Nevada, at about 9:00 that morning for a doctor's appointment in Sacramento, California. She would later pick up her husband, a pilot, in San Jose. By her side, sat quiet little Leo, her constant companion. "He was my baby, my surrogate child. I loved him very much. I had had him for ten years before he was killed," she told me.

"I had never been in San Jose before, and it was raining heavily the entire trip. Traffic was in gridlock at the airport, and I was having trouble getting into a directional lane to my left. Out of the blue, this guy came flying around me in a black SUV on my right, cut in front of me, and into the lane I had been trying to get into." Moments later, Sara bumped this guy by accident. "It was a very slight tap, no damage at all. The next thing I knew, this guy was out of his vehicle and approaching my car," she continued.

"I have a window that goes all the way down once you hit the down button. Before I knew it, Leo had awaken and was on my lap. He wasn't barking, just sitting there on my lap quietly looking up at this guy. Leo loved people and always greeted them in a friendly way. To him, this guy was just another human to meet. Just another stranger who might give him a dog biscuit.

This guy said something to me, then reached in with both arms and grabbed Leo and turned around. I thought he was trying to kidnap him, but instead, he threw Leo out into the oncoming traffic lanes. I jumped out to run after him, but then realized that I had left my car in drive and it had lurched forward into the black SUV. I ran back to my car and put it into park. When I ran back to help Leo, a car ran over him right in front of me before I could grab him."

Sara went on to tell me how she cradled Leo in her arms and put him on her car seat. She called 911 and got the number of an emergency veterinarian, but since she was not familiar with the town, it meant nothing to her. She frantically ran into the terminal and found her husband. They were able to reach a vet, who guided them to the hospital, but by the time they arrived, Leo had died in her arms. "Nobody ever loved a dog more than I loved Leo," Sara said. "But his death has caused people from all over the U.S. to donate money to animal shelters, adopt pets, and many other wonderful things. He has left behind quite a legacy for such a little dog."

Sara confirmed with me that the reward for identifying Leo's killer is well over $100,000 at the time of this writing. Apparently, if caught, he could be convicted of felony animal cruelty, receive up to one year in jail, be fined up to $20,000, and also face a battery of other charges, such as leaving the scene of an accident.

When I asked Sara if she had any advice for other motorists, she recommended that if you are a woman driving alone, "Never open your car window to a stranger."

Sara's husband Patrick and her mother, Dr. Marilyn McGovern MD, recently surprised her with a little package. "Stormy," another little male Bichon Frise, now keeps Sara company and occupies the co-pilot seat next to her.

Rest in peace, little Leo. Here's hoping the authorities get this cruel idiot and prosecute him to the fullest.

Leo

Sara and Leo

Chapter Nine

Under Attack: Bicyclists

Bicyclists across the U.S. are often victims, and on occasion, the instigators of road rage, though few of us ever think much about it. We're not talking about accidents here. Accidents involving motorists and bicycles do happen, where one party or the other simply makes a driving or riding mistake. However, as bicycling continues to grow in popularity, clashes between motorists and bicyclists today are increasingly more hostile and violent.

Over 5 million Americans ride their bikes to school or work every day. Surveys indicate that another 20 million say that they would do so if it were safer. There is no doubt that the popularity of cycling has grown by leaps and bounds in the U.S.

Sadly, though, every year about 840 cyclists are killed by motor vehicles. Another 75,000 are injured in collisions between bicycles and motor vehicles. Judging from news stories and discussions on the Internet, as well as cyclists' opinions, road rage incidents involving cyclists and vehicles are on the rise.[34]

Many cyclists I spoke with talked of being harassed repeatedly. "They'll throw soda cans at you, beer bottles, you name it," said one cyclist. "They'll cuss you out for being in the road, spit on you, and scream bloody murder. They just don't feel we have a right to be out here. Drivers just seem to want to hassle you for the fun of it."

According to Dave Hixon, an acquaintance of mine and leader of a local cyclist club, few motorists understand that bicyclists, by law, have every right to be on the road with other traffic, with the exception of interstate highways.

"I once had a guy pull over in a fit of fury and start giving me a hard time about being on the road with my bike. He was going on and on about how bikes are for the sidewalks and cars are for the roads, and that I didn't have a right to be on the roads. I told him that Missouri state law allows bikes on the road, and that in fact, bicycles are covered in the driver's testing handbook the state gives out. He didn't believe me, but he just happened to have one in his glove compartment. He retrieved it, and I showed him the section on bicycles, at which he mumbled a few words and drove off," Dave said.

Apparently, drivers will pull right out in front of cyclists without hesitation and with little regard. "It really can get dangerous out there," Dave commented. "You have to constantly be scanning all around you for danger. One of the worst problems is drivers getting right behind you. Some of them will play a game by seeing just how close they can get to you from behind. You know that if you fall, you don't have a chance."

But Dave also went on to say that it's a two way street. "As a cyclist club leader, I tell every cyclist I meet that we must obey the rules of the road. It goes both ways. If cyclists themselves will try harder to behave and not provoke drivers, that will help us all," he said. I couldn't agree more. If you are a cyclist, first, watch out for yourself, and second, don't provoke anger from drivers. In today's world, it doesn't always mean much if you're right. Being right won't save you from being run over. An arrogant attitude can get you killed, and killed fast!

London England Woman Jailed for Running Down Cyclist

Anger and aggression behind the wheel, are not limited by age, gender, or social status. Take the case of Frances Cernuschi.[35]

Ms. Cernuschi was a 46-year-old $60,000-per-year stock broker from Tooting, in south London, England. A very successful career woman, she literally went berserk when a cyclist scratched her car one day as he rode past her on the street.

According to court records, on August 15, 1997, she

became enraged when a medical student, Alexander Wade, accidentally bumped into her Rover on his bicycle. Police and witnesses said that she then proceeded to attempt to run him down. She apparently accelerated her 4,000 pound car and went after Mr. Wade, 21. Catching up to him, she reportedly swerved into him, knocking him down.

The case, heard in Southwark Crown Court, was presided over by Judge Peter Fingret. During her sentencing, Judge Fingret stated that she had used her 4,000 pound car "as a weapon."

"This was a deliberate act of dangerous driving by you to give a cyclist what you described as a 'glancing blow' to tell him 'don't you dare do it again.' It was a deliberate assault by you using your car as a weapon on an innocent road user," the Judge said. He went on to say her crime was aggravated by a "cold and callous" decision to drive away after knocking Mr. Wade onto the road. Apparently, she had driven over his wheel, just missing his leg. Judge Fingret said it was "sheer luck" that Mr. Wade was not seriously injured. He escaped with only minor cuts and bruises. The judge continued by stating, "Incidents like this are committed by selfish and reckless motorists."

Ian Parsons, a witness to the attack, chased Mrs. Cernuschi on his motorcycle and reported her license plate number to police. He was later given 100 pounds by the court for assisting in her apprehension.

Mrs. Cernuschi was sentenced to five months in jail, and in an unusual decision, her car was impounded and sold. During her defense, her lawyer said that she had been frightened when Mr. Wade struck her car with his bike and had reacted angrily, but that her anger quickly turned to panic as she drove off.

Her employer, Charles Stanley, Ltd., vowed to give her job back when her jail term was up. She will likely need it, since she'll have to buy another car and quite possibly, still have to pay off the Rover she used in the attack.

Bad Cyclists

Having spent over two years driving through the clogged streets of New York City, I personally witnessed both sides of cyclist behavior. Many cyclists were very well behaved. However, some of them were lightening fast terrors!

One common bad trait was the cyclists' habit of flying between the tight lanes of cars as we sat in idle traffic. They would come from all angles, swerving and darting right and left around our cars. Most of us didn't mind that so much. After all, no use being envious of those who can keep moving if you can't.

However, after a few years of enduring cyclists using their feet to push off of your car door or fender to change directions, or hanging onto your mirrors or rear tire carrier as you head down the road because they're tired of peddling and want a free ride, you begin to get a little jaded. They would come out of nowhere, startle you by glancing off your car, rocking it suddenly, and sometimes causing damage. A good number of these cyclists were couriers, ferrying mail and packages between office buildings within the city.

As a result of this behavior and other factors, such as vehicle theft, most commuters I knew, drove old vehicles to work and left their good cars at home. Some had what they referred to as their "Yankee Stadium car." It had no radio in it to *steal (no fancy features that would excite a thief)* and was worth little. Many of these drivers didn't even lock the doors.

The theory was that a thief could open the door and look around without breaking the windows. These cars also allowed the cyclists and the occasional *roller blader* to kick off of them while changing directions, grab the mirrors, or what have you, without the owners caring too much. When you live or work in New York, you just learn to cope.

Of course, these bike bandits of the big city knew that catching them was a near impossibility, since they would always be moving so fast, and you're not about to get out of your car to chase them and leave it running in New York. *(There were stories of retribution, where commuters would open their car doors just as a cyclist would come by: ouch!).*

So, there are times when cyclists themselves provoke motorists into retaliation and make a bad name for themselves with some drivers. At other times, completely innocent cyclists, minding their own business, are often attacked with little or no provocation at all.

Biking Can be Dangerous

The states with the worst records for biking safety are Florida, with 8.8 deaths per year per million; Arizona, with 7.0; Louisiana, with 5.9; and South Carolina, with 5.4 deaths per million. The safest states are Rhode Island, with 1.1 deaths per million per year; West Virginia, with 1.2; and New Hampshire, with 1.6 deaths per million. In essence, then, a cyclist is about eight times more likely to be killed in a collision with a vehicle in Florida than in Rhode Island.[36]

Many Cities Opt for Bike Lanes

Albuquerque, New Mexico, is just one city that is trying to accommodate cyclists by making commuting and recreational cycling safer. Since 1992, the number of bike trails and lanes has doubled in and around the city. An astonishing 239 miles of bikeways now traverse the city, according to city planners. More miles of bikeways are also being planned. Some bikers in the city travel 60 or 70 miles or more by bike trail every day.

Denver, Chicago, and other cities are following suit by adding biking trails and bike lanes for cyclists. It appears that separating cyclists and motorists, albeit expensive, has been effective in reducing tension between the two and will undoubtedly help reduce injuries and fatalities. Those who are physically able to bike to work not only get their daily dose of exercise, but they're doing their part to reduce congestion and emissions as well.

For the cyclists out there who still must mix it up with motorists, take the advice of Dave Hixon and others: keep a sharp eye out for yourself. There are some crazy drivers out there who'll take you out in a heartbeat, a few of them with little, if any, remorse. Forget about being right, and stay alive! In a later chapter on road rage prevention, we discuss ways to protect yourself from becoming a statistic.

Chapter Ten

The Amish Under Attack

There are no more peaceful people on earth then the Amish. Having spent a week among these shy, reclusive folks in Pennsylvania as a young 18 year-old, this author learned to appreciate their strange, but peace-loving ways. After suffering decades of severe persecution in Europe, they, like others around the world, sought refuge here in North America. Once here, they flourished and found in the American people the tolerance they had prayed for.

Like throwbacks to the 18th century, they keep a religion and customs that allow them to use very few modern day conveniences. When it comes to transportation, very few of them own automobiles. Instead, they still ply the roadways around their communities in horse-drawn wagons and buggies. There are a few of the Amish who drive vehicles or ride bicycles, but the preferred method of transportation is still the horse.

There is a community of Amish and Mennonites in northern Missouri and southern Iowa, not far from where I live, but the majority of their number live in and around Indiana, Ohio, and Pennsylvania.

Any one of us who has had to slow down to pass a horse drawn buggy on a two-lane highway will agree that such an encounter can be a slight aggravation. This is especially true if we're in a hurry. However, it is hard to imagine anyone losing their cool and deliberately attacking these peaceful people.

Well, imagine or not, it's happening. Police agencies are reporting that attacks on Amish people are increasing in number and seriousness. Worse, due to their religion and forgiving nature, many of these attacks are not being reported to authorities.

Men Attack Amish Cyclists with Tire Irons!

In one of the most despicable acts to date against the peaceful Amish, a group of five men decided that Amish men would make good target practice. In 1996, these five men from Northern Indiana decided that the Amish presented an easy target, especially those who ride their bicycles along the side of the road. In a series of violent assaults, these brave heroes would drive up behind the Amish men as they rode their bikes and hit them with *tire irons*. Yes, tire irons! Once the victim was incapacitated, these heroes would then stop, jump out of their vehicles, and rob them.[37]

Although even young Amish boys are usually well conditioned and powerfully strong from years of back-breaking labor in the fields, and well capable of defending themselves, they will not strike back. To them, amazingly, to strike back at an attacker is considered "weak."

Professor Bryan Byers

I contacted Associate Professor Bryan Byers of Ball State University's Department of Criminal Justice, Muncie, Indiana, and discussed the assaults with him. Professor Byers has studied crimes against the Amish for some time. As part of his research, he has questioned hundreds of Amish and non-Amish alike, in an effort to better understand the phenomenon.

"Abuse of the Amish people, including on the roadways, is very common around Amish communities," Prof. Byers said. "The Amish are seen as easy targets due to their peaceful, forgiving nature. Amazingly, when an attack or confrontation occurs, most of them want to know what *they* did wrong and how they can change what they are doing to prevent another conflict. They feel that surely they must have done something to provoke the attack. A Bishop I spoke with wanted to know how they as a community could learn to avoid provoking such attacks. He just couldn't grasp the idea that there are people around them who are evil enough to attack them for no obvious reason. It's amazing."

"The vast majority of people like the Amish," continued Professor Byers. "However, the younger people are the biggest offenders," he said. "It's always been that way, though. Some of the younger boys see the Amish as stupid, backward, etc. It's sort of like eighteenth century vs. twentieth century, if you will."

Buggy Bashing

In an aside from the Amish bicycle attacks, Professor Byers went on to discuss with me how the Amish are also being hassled while driving their buggies on the roads.

"There are a number of problems that raise their ugly heads when it comes to Amish buggies and modern vehicles sharing the same road," he said. "One of the most prevalent is the fact that buggies are obviously not as controllable as modern cars. After all, there is a horse in front. An animal. Consequently, buggies sometimes take longer to stop, and when it comes to stop signs and turns, the buggy drivers are many times not able to stop at all. The buggies will sometimes whip out in front of a car from seemingly nowhere, upsetting motorists. They are not nearly as controllable or predictable as cars."

In another example of frustration that results from the difference between the buggy and the automobile, Prof. Byers went on to discuss equestrian "poop" as a source of irritation. "I talked with two people who were absolutely convinced that the Amish had their horses drop manure in the road just to irritate them. One lady was certain that the buggy drivers would have their horses wait until she got directly behind them, and they would then somehow signal them to poop, causing her to run through the slop and mess-up her car," he said. *(OK Trigger, we've got a live one behind us..... let her rip, boy!).*

Wow, the imagination that some people have! I've had horses around off and on for years, and "poop response" training is something that just isn't possible with a horse or mule. These are not house-breakable pets. I do suppose there are some horse ignorant people out there who think a horse is just like their pet tabby cat, or poodle, and can be trained to poop on command. Maybe the Amish could start helping themselves by teaching the general public about the front and back ends of a horse!

Prof. Byers also held focus groups in Shipshewana, Indiana, with Amish and other locals, and during special sessions, he conducted interviews with people who had been convicted of crimes against Amish people. "They had no remorse. Even years after high school, they still didn't feel that running a buggy off the road, cussing, or abusing the Amish was any big deal."

Prof. Byers also said that occasionally there are problems that occur when Amish men spit chewing tobacco out of their buggies. Even if the tobacco doesn't hit a person or a car, many see it as disrespectful to them and take offense.

Apparently, drivers sometimes play a game of "chicken" with the buggies as they try to get as close to them as possible. Stories of spooked horses and out-of-control buggies are not uncommon. Beer bottles, cans, rocks, and other items are sometimes thrown at the horses in an attempt to cause a run away. Such is the state of mind of some folks "just out to have some fun."

There are good and bad drivers out there, but as far as the joy-seekers who pick on the peaceful Amish are concerned, hitting them, trying to injure them, etc., this author sees them as some of the lowest cowards in the world. Get a life, guys.

On the positive side, some communities are building "buggy lanes" similar to biking trails to separate the buggies from motor vehicles. Time will tell if these lanes become widespread. On the surface, separating rudimentary eighteenth century travel from today's swift twentieth century transportation looks like a grand idea.

Horse Riders are Being Assaulted

It's worthy of note that a friend of mine, Dave, also rides his horse along a two-lane highway near his home, here, in Missouri. Over the years, he has had the same treatment as the Amish.

Hell-bent idiots will come by and honk, throw objects, peel out to throw gravel at him and his horse, scream, cut him off, and do other things to try and spook his horse, risking both the horse and rider's safety. To these idiots, it's just having fun.

On one occasion, however, this friend of mine was ready for them. He strapped on his .357 magnum before riding this particular evening, knowing that the same idiots who had harassed him for days as he rode would likely be back. Sure enough, just as it was getting dark, here they came, and a beer bottle whizzed by his head, missing him by only inches. As the car turned around to make another pass, Dave quickly dismounted and drew the revolver. As they came near, window rolled down, Dave shot several volleys over the top of the car. (Note: there were no houses on the opposite side of the road.) Obviously, the guys in the car, thinking that they were sure to meet St. Peter at any moment, took off in a big hurry, and quite possibly soiled their jeans.

You may not agree with Dave's "old west justice" solution to this type of "equestrian road rage," but it was none-the-less effective. He never saw the car again.

Chapter Eleven

Highway Workers Being Assaulted

Highway Worker Faces Ax Attack by Motorist

Across the U.S., one of the most hazardous jobs is that of roadway repair crews. Every so often, a motorist, either driving too fast, under the influence, or for some other reason, loses control and injures or kills a road repair worker. However, what happened to Jimmy Hall, a West Virginia state highway equipment operator, and a coworker was something his safety training had not prepared him for in the least.

While Hall was fixing potholes on Highway 250 near Charleston, West Virginia, an enraged driver leaped from his car, grabbed an ax, and lunged forward toward Hall's coworker, who had been using a flag to warn motorists to slow their speed as they approached the construction zone.[38]

Reportedly, the ax-wielding driver stopped just short of the flagman, backed off, and dropped the ax. He then returned to his car and left the area. The work crew was stunned to say the least. Hall and the crew later said that it *"happened so fast."* They also said that they now look over their shoulders constantly while working.

Some Workers are Being Killed

In Connecticut alone, 13 highway workers have died since 1992. Of these, five were killed by job hazards while the other eight were struck by traffic. A few years ago, Connecticut, like other states, doubled the fines for speeding in construction zones. However, workers have recently complained that the stricter law is being largely ignored and not enforced.[39]

As stated elsewhere in this book, the following stories help to illustrate the apparent lack of concern for our fellow man out there on the roads. Aggressive drivers are lashing out at highway workers as they struggle to repair potholes on our roads. Ironically, these workers are being assaulted and in some cases, run over as they try to fix these vehicle-damaging and accident-causing road hazards for us.

In an article published in the *Hartford Courant*, several highway workers shared their thoughts and harrowing stories of near-death encounters with angry motorists.

"My Orange Vest Was Ripped from My Back"

Anthony Frattallone was working on a road repair crew on I-95 in Connecticut. It happened so fast that there was no time to get out of the way, nor to break free. "The only thing that saved me was my partner yelling at me," said Frattallone. "All I could do was jump out of the way and arch my back as I felt my vest being torn off by a passing motorist."

Fred Schaeffer recalled seeing the orange flag being ripped out of the hand of a flagger trying to direct traffic.

Assaulted with Flying Objects

According to Lee Turner, also a Connecticut DOT worker, drivers will throw just about anything at them as the speed past his road crew. "Bottles, banana peels, tea bags...they swear at you and give you the finger. If you want to see an example of road rage, come to a highway work zone," he said.

In April, 1999, an agreement called "Operation Big Orange" was reached between the unions and state troopers to make highway work-zone safety a priority. This agreement includes hidden radar guns mounted in road repair trucks to catch aggressive drivers.

Part Two

The Many Causes of Road Rage

In part two, we examine the many possible causes of road rage from the commuter's point of view. While leaders and traffic experts around the world dig deep into the issues in search of answers, to the average commuter on the street, the causes of road rage aren't really all that hard to understand. Boiled down to its simplest elements, without all the lofty psychological terminology and million-dollar words, my research into this phenomenon revealed that road rage is usually caused by drivers who fall into two general categories.

1. Regardless of age or position in life. Many people are under extreme mental pressure, either acute *(momentarily)* at the scene of the road rage event,

or chronic *(over a period of time)*, as the Athnos tractor-trailer attempted murder case revealed.

2. The second category of road rager, is the driver who displays repeated, habitual anger and rage in many areas of their life, not just in their driving. Many of these drivers have prior criminal records and exhibit spousal abuse, drug use, and other antisocial behavior. These people care little about the rights and lives of others, especially when they're behind the wheel.

We will look at both the "acute" road rager, the usually calm, courteous driver, who just seems to lose it at the wrong time, and the more habitual bad guys of the road. We will also look into what federal, state, and local governments are doing to help stem the tide of road rage.

As you continue to read through this book, remember this: today in North America, we can't seem to build enough prisons. We're locking people up in record numbers. It seems criminals are everywhere. They must be, right? They're found in every hamlet and town across this great land.

This being said, ask yourself one question: where were all these "bad" people before they went to the big house? The answer is obvious: That were out there with you on the roads...and there are others out there with you every day. Be wise, and be careful out there on the highways and back roads. That guy or gal in the car next to you or hugging your rear bumper could be just a neighbor in a hurry, or a very dangerous individual who could care less if you live or die. Play it safe, and get out of their way!

Chapter Twelve

The National Highway Traffic Safety Administration

Road Rage Gets Federal Attention

The National Highway Traffic Safety Administration (NHTSA) has begun to address the problem of road rage and aggressive driving at the national level. As cries for help from the states echoed through the halls of NHTSA, top bureaucrats at the agency began to take notice. The agency has begun to try and get the word out through a series of brochures, meetings with concerned citizens, and by voicing their concerns before special congressional committees.

On July 17, 1997, NHTSA sent out a news release which described details of a House Surface Transportation Subcommittee hearing the agency attended on the same day. The hearing concerned continued funding for NHTSA, and was held at the Rayburn House Office Building. During this hearing, the Subcommittee heard testimony from some of the leading road rage experts in the nation, all of whom supported continued funding of the agency.[40]

NHTSA officials and supporters took the opportunity to discuss injury and accident statistics, and to express their opinions on the current magnitude of the road rage and aggressive driving problem.

According to the news release, the following issues were discussed at length during the hearing:

- **Causes of aggressive driving.**

- **The danger aggressive driving and road rage presents to the public.**

- **Actions that are being taken, or may be taken, to combat this problem.**

Appearing before the Subcommittee in addition to the experts from (NHTSA), were experts from the Automobile Association of America (AAA), the Insurance Institute for Highway Safety, and other safety and advocacy groups. In addition, several psychologists who specialize in the treatment of aggressive driving gave testimony.

The discussions focused on the perceived causes of aggressive driving and road rage, ongoing research to further understand the growing problem, the various enforcement measures in place, and available options for federal initiatives to address the problems.

The following are NHTSA's observations and comments on road rage, which they expressed at the subcommittee meeting. Since NHTSA is the leading *federal* agency involved with protection of the public on America's highways, their opinions and actions are of major significance to the states. Mr. Jesse Blatt, an administrator for the agency, was very helpful in conveying NHTSA's stance on this important issue to this author.

The Experts Speak Out
NHTSA's Ricardo Martinez, M.D.

At the time of this writing, Ricardo Martinez, M.D., was the Administrator at the National Highway Safety Traffic Agency. On July 17, 1997, Dr. Martinez, along with other distinguished experts in the field, spoke before the U.S. House of Representatives Subcommittee on Transportation and Infrastructure. The purpose of the meeting was to discuss the problem of aggressive driving and it's impact on the nation.

Dr. Martinez detailed statistics, which, if correct, lend credibility to the perception that our nation's roads are indeed becoming more violent and dangerous.

"To place the problem of aggressive driving in context, let me begin by mentioning several facts about the nation's highway safety picture," Dr. Martinez said.

He then stated the following facts:

- Highway fatalities have decreased from 50,984 in 1966 to 41,907 in 1996 despite an enormous increase in travel.

- The fatality rate decreased by 69% during this period, from 5.5 fatalities per hundred million miles traveled to 1.7, an all time low.

- Alcohol involvement in fatal crashes has dropped from 57% to 41% over this same 15 year period. Seat belt use has grown from 11% in 1982 to 68% in 1996.

- Truck-related fatalities continue to decrease despite an increase in truck travel and a 170% increase in the number of drivers holding commercial driver's licenses.

- Rail-highway grade crossing fatalities at public crossings have also decreased by 31% over the last seven years (1990-1996).

- Since 1992, seat belts, child safety seats, motorcycle helmets, and the age-21 minimum drinking age laws have saved over 40,000 lives.

- Elimination of highway roadway hazards has saved an estimated 6,200 lives.

- An estimated 1,700 lives have been saved through rail-highway crossing improvement programs.

That's the good news, according to Dr. Martinez. "After years of steady decline," Martinez continued, "highway deaths increased slightly over the last four years."

According to the agency, 41,907 people died in 1996, and over three million were injured in police-reported crashes. Dr. Martinez went on to say that although the nation's fatality rate remains low, these highway crashes still cost the country $150.5 billion per year.

"We estimate that about one-third of these crashes and about two-thirds of the resulting fatalities can be attributed to behavior associated with aggressive driving," said Martinez.

Definitions of Aggressive Driving Vary

According to Mr. Blatt, of NHTSA, there is no universal or standard definition of road rage. However, a consensus has begun to take shape. Most academic researchers now define road rage as:

An incident in which an angry or impatient motorist or passenger intentionally injures or kills another motorist, passenger, or pedestrian, or attempts to injure or kill in response to a traffic dispute, altercation, or grievance.

Aggressive driving is generally seen as speeding, rapid and sudden lane changes, etc., but without intent to harm or assault, and without gestures, glances, etc.

NHTSA says that the general public tends to view aggressive driving and road rage as any type of risk-taking behavior behind the wheel, including speeding, tailgating, weaving dangerously through traffic, and ignoring stop signs or red lights.

"While the media focuses on the more horrific incidents described by the academic definition of aggressive driving, it is the general risk-taking behavior behind the wheel that is more prevalent and appears to result in far more deaths and injuries," says NHTSA.

According to NHTSA, some researchers believe there is a growing trend of simple aggressive behavior. These incidents include angry reactions to other drivers, i.e., honking, tailgating, gesturing, and cutting them off.

A recent study conducted by the AAA Foundation for Traffic Safety found that nearly 90% of drivers have experienced an aggressive driving incident in the past 12 months (using the public's definition of aggressive driving). The AAA study also concluded that since 1990, aggressive driving incidents have increased by an estimated 51%, resulting in an average of 1,500 fatalities and injuries each year.

NHTSA also stated that in the Washington, DC, metropolitan area, aggressive driving has reached such epidemic proportions that motorists rank it ahead of drunk driving among their concerns.

Causes

NHTSA:

"Aggressive driving itself is not a new phenomenon. However, attention has only recently been focused on aggressive driving as a national problem. Researchers believe that aggressive driving is more than an action; it is a behavioral pattern. As with most behaviors, it arises from a culmination of overlapping factors. *While some personality types may have a propensity for aggressive driving behaviors, given the right circumstances, anyone can fall victim.*

"Congestion is the leading cause of aggressive driving. According to the Federal Highway Administration, almost 70% of urban freeways are now congested as opposed to 55% in 1983. The amount of vehicle miles traveled since 1987 has increased by 35%, whereas miles of road increased by only 1%. In the past decade, the number of cars has grown faster than the population. Very slow or stationary traffic situations present conditions which may trigger driver aggression. Some of the worst cases of aggressive driving have occurred where the opportunity for vehicles to separate and go their own way does not present itself. A study reported that psychologists believe that increasingly crowded highways and busier schedules have made drivers more frantic and hostile.

"Some researchers also contend that traffic induced aggression stems in part from territorial defensiveness. The car is often considered an extension of *personal space*. People become contentious when someone encroaches on that private territory with action such as cutting them off or bumping them from behind. In Colorado Springs, a 55-year-old man persuaded a 17-year-old boy who had been tailgating him to pull off to the side of the road. An argument ensued and instead of reprimanding him, he fatally shot the boy. Some researchers believe that higher safety standards and features in automobiles, such as anti-lock braking systems, give motorists a greater sense of invulnerability. With this inflated sense of safety, they may take more chances on the road and thereby drive more aggressively.

"Americans also increasingly try to fit more into their already busy schedules. When there is a perception of impeded progress, an intuitive response follows. This instinctive response may include anything from the flashing of lights to something more combative. On urban streets, pedestrians are injured by aggressive and unaggressive drivers. Nearly 100,000 pedestrians are injured in motor vehicle accidents each year in the United States, with a majority of these accidents taking place in urban areas."

An International Problem

Mr. Blatt also talked with me about several road rage studies now being performed by different organizations and private individuals, some of them outside the U.S. Apparently, the phenomenon of road rage isn't limited to the United States. We discuss some of the foreign road rage issues in later chapters.

Traffic violence and behavioral studies are going on in other countries as well. As smaller, third-world countries accumulate more wealth and buying power, they buy more cars. As their standard of living increases, their ability to purchase automobiles becomes a reality. However, few of these countries have the road systems to handle such an increase in traffic volume. The result is predictable. We also look at some of these issues later in this book.

Ongoing Research

According to Jim McKnight, a researcher with the National Public Services Research Institute, research on road rage is sparse. As one who has spent many hours combing through stacks of traffic accident data, Mr. McKnight should know.

"The primary problem in regard to data on highway violence is the lack of a good nationwide system for collecting and disseminating data on traffic incidents that involve violence," said McKnight. "Most municipal, county, and state law enforcement agencies use traffic ticketing systems that do not have specific, defined categories for traffic violence listed on their forms.

"Most of the information is very brief and consists primarily of diagrams, brief statements about vehicle travel direction at the point of impact, etc. The information remains very static and un-descriptive in regard to road violence," said Mr. McKnight.

"Even if they did have such categories, they might be reluctant to use them. The truth is, we may never see a reliable system of this type that would allow us to compile good statistical data at the national level. Most efforts to compile reliable statistics and to analyze the problem from a statistical viewpoint remain at the local, grass roots level. For the time being, newspapers are probably the best source of nationwide data gathering, at least from the standpoint of accumulating data on the most grievous traffic violence. These horrific accidents and affronts to civilized society usually make the headlines," he said.

"However," McKnight continued, "NHTSA and others are engaged in gathering statistical data on highway violence using phone surveys, questionnaires, and other accepted methods. These studies may prove to be very useful in determining the magnitude of the problem, at least as seen through the eyes of the public."

Chapter Thirteen

The "Road Rage Detail"
The Illinois State Police Fight Back

The Illinois State Police have established one of the finest and most successful road rage fighting programs in the nation. Frustrated by ever-growing injuries, fatalities, and a complete disregard by some drivers for the safety and rights of others on Illinois highways, a pair of Illinois State Troopers decided it was time to fight back.

Master Sergeant Paul Stokes and Sergeant Troy Lewis, with 26 and 24 years of police service, respectively, are Illinois State Police veterans. Frustrated in their efforts to catch road ragers, they saw a need to try something different. They agreed that a special traffic safety unit dedicated solely to the issue of road rage was what they really needed to make Illinois roads safer.

In 1996, they sent their suggestion for the special unit to the Director's Office in Springfield and waited for a favorable response. "We really saw a serious problem here in District 11," says M/Sgt. Stokes. "We felt we had to do something radical...something different from the traditional police procedures we had been using. We had to find unconventional ways of apprehending these dangerous drivers."

Apparently, Sergeants Stokes and Lewis made a good case to their superiors. Terrance Gainer, at the time Director of the Illinois State Police, approved the idea as a pilot program. The Road Rage Detail was born. With a limited budget, Stokes and Lewis were charged with outfitting and directing the activities of the new experimental unit. Besides Stokes and Lewis, two full time troopers are assigned to the unit. The other two troopers are Trooper Ignacio Escobedo and Trooper Floyd Smith. Both are very aggressive, hard working troopers.

The Learning Curve

"At first, we used our traditional patrol cars in our Road Rage Detail efforts," M/Sgt. Stokes explained. "But these offensive-minded drivers are smart. They are constantly scanning the road ahead, looking for us. The lights on top of our cars and the police paint schemes are a dead giveaway from quite a distance.

"We then started using unmarked patrol cars. This helped a lot, but we were still having trouble catching many of the worst offenders. As I said before, these drivers are constantly scanning the road ahead, and they get very good at seeing us before we can catch them. We had to find a more covert approach to the problem.

"Across the country, most drivers know the typical makes and models of vehicles used by law enforcement agencies. Road ragers readily pick out these conventional police cars, like the Ford Crown Victoria and Chevrolet Caprice, and hit their brakes before we can get a fix on them.

"Finally, we borrowed a covert unit [detective vehicle]. These cars are outfitted with police dash strobe lights and flashing headlights. For example, we've had a lot of success with a sporty black Monte Carlo. The look of shock on the faces of these dangerous violators when they're pulled over by a trooper in an ordinary looking Chevy says it all. It's an extremely effective approach."

Impressive Statistics

"From November 17, 1997, through the end of March, 1998, we made 1,545 driving arrests and issued 189 warnings to violators," Stokes said.

"The warnings were for ancillary, non-traffic violation problems such as broken taillights, expired plates, etc. We do not issue warnings to violators who break the safety rules of the road (weavers, tailgaters, etc.). Nor do we issue warnings for not wearing a seat belt. It's either on or off, no exceptions. We want people to survive a crash should tragic misfortune find them on our highways.

"Aggressive, dangerous drivers, when caught by our Road Rage Detail, *will walk away with a fist full of tickets*," said Stokes. "We want them to know that. What we're looking for is voluntary compliance. We want people using the highways in the State of Illinois to obey peaceably our highway traffic safety laws. We're in the business of protecting and serving those who use our multilane and two lane highway systems. It's our job and we take it very seriously," he said.

Judging from the figures, the Illinois State Road Rage Detail is working beyond expectations. The program has passed the pilot program test. It is now a fully funded program that is here to stay, according to Stokes. "Or at least until it's no longer needed," the sergeant explained. "The program is fully supported from the top down. From the Governor's Office and our State Police Director right down to the line officers. The support for our efforts has been outstanding."

When I asked both M/Sgt. Stokes and Sergeant Lewis if there was anyone else from the legal profession I could talk to about the program, such as prosecuting attorneys or state's attorneys in their area, they hesitated. "Not really," was their joint reply. "We have not had *even one* road rage violator challenge us in court. Like we said, they know they're in trouble when we catch them. It's very hard to explain your way out of a road rage type ticket. We do not pull drivers over until we have ample cause and justification to do so. The local and state judiciary, including the prosecutors and judges, have come on board with us. They are taking a very hard stance against this type of behavior. They're sick of it too."

What if a Driver Refuses to Pull Over?

When we discussed the possibility of a driver not pulling over in distrust (a cop in a Camaro?), Sergeant Stokes explained their procedure.

"We discussed the possibility of this scenario happening. Should this situation arise, our procedures call for us to request a marked patrol car to assist us. We will simply back off a safe distance and wait for the marked patrol car to arrive and pull the driver over. However, to date, we have not had to do this. The unconventional cars are equipped with flashing headlights and inside mounted red and blue strobe lights. *And once we put on the hat, they know they're caught and they pull over.*"

A Typical Road Rager Profile

"We're arresting aggressive drivers from all walks of life," said Sergeant Stokes. "The typical profile tells you that most of the offenders are single males between the ages of 16 and 25. That may be true on the whole, but we've arrested grandmothers, parents with their kids in their cars, farmers, businessmen, you name it. One team member even ticketed a nun!

"Social status or ethnic background doesn't matter either. Rich, poor, or in between, we've arrested aggressive drivers from all walks of life.

"People are busier nowadays. The pace of life is faster. People just get in too much of a hurry and endanger themselves as well as others on the roadways."

"However, there are some drivers out there who go beyond aggressive. They can get very violent, even deadly.

We are trying to get these people off the road," said the sergeant.

Those Who Drive too Slow

I asked Sergeants Stokes and Lewis about some of the sources of road rage, *drivers who cause other drivers to get angry:*

- Drivers who drive slow in the passing lane and refuse to get over.

- Drivers who come to a complete stop on merging-traffic ramps from overpasses.

- Drivers who don't use their turn signals.

- Drivers who can't seem to function properly on the roadway, making them a danger to themselves and others.

"When we encounter a driver who seems to be unaware of the rules of the road, or in some way may be a danger to themselves and others on the road, we become very concerned for their safety. This is sometimes apparent with the elderly, but includes other drivers as well. If we feel strongly enough that a driver may need to be retested, we can request that they be retested by the Illinois Secretary of State. We don't like to do it, but it's part of our responsibility in law enforcement," said M/Sgt. Stokes.

Cell Phones

I also commented to Sergeants Stokes and Lewis about cell phone usage, and asked them their opinions on the subject.

At times, it seems that almost half the drivers I see in traffic are on their cell phones. *I've gotten pretty good at picking them out from a distance: They drive too slow, too fast, and quite often, a little of both. Their minds are not on their driving, so they speed up and slow down constantly, as their minds wander from the call back to the road, etc.*

"For a trooper, that's a little bit of a tough one," replied Stokes. "We have cell phones in our patrol cars, too. We would prefer that people pull over or wait until they stop to use their cell phones. It can get tricky when people are concentrating on the call and not the road. Since these phones are here to stay, we'll all just have to continue to deal with them."

Model for a Frustrated Nation

The Illinois State Police Road Rage Detail has caught the eye of frustrated law enforcement agencies across the nation.

Lieutenant Ken Carter serves on the Illinois State Police Aggressive Driving Committee, at the State Police Headquarters in Springfield. Lt. Carter says he is receiving quite a few requests for information on their successful Road Rage Detail.

"We've had inquiries from US News, The National Safety Council, Washington State, and others. We're also providing information to a number of police training facilities," Carter said.

A Ride in a "Stealth Patrol Car"

During my early road rage discussions with Sergeants Stokes and Lewis, they invited me to ride along with them and observe their Road Rage Detail operation first hand. I jumped at the opportunity. What better way to understand how police are coping with the problem than by observing it all from their vantage point?

After receiving approval from Lieutenant Charles Brueggemann, commander of District III State Police, it was time to climb into a sporty black '96 Monte Carlo with Sgt. Lewis at the wheel, and hang on.

June 30, 1998. It's 8:00am when I arrive at District 11 Headquarters. Lewis and Stokes greet me and make me feel right at home. Lean, fit, and immaculately attired in their military style uniforms, their neat appearance embodies the proud, professional organization they belong too. *(I can't help but remember my Air Force Basic training days. They look an awful lot like my old Drill Instructors!)* However, they quickly put me at ease as we discuss their Road Rage Detail operations. These are two genuinely nice guys who just happen to be troopers. No bull, no bravado. Just down-to-earth, warm professionals.

After a short discussion covering the morning's agenda, it's time to buckle up and observe road rage from a trooper's perspective.

0827 hrs: Sgt. Lewis spots a car ahead changing lanes rapidly. He speeds up, but the driver slows down and exits the highway before we can catch up. "We have to be careful what we're doing out here in these covert cars," Sgt. Lewis says. "The other drivers around us don't know that we're troopers, either. We want to catch the bad guys, but at the same time, we can't endanger the other drivers out here."

"I routinely catch drivers doing 80 to 90 miles per hour plus out here," the Sgt. Continues. "I've clocked two drivers at *102 miles per hour* on one stretch of road," he said.

Playing Chicken

"It's dangerous out here. Some people just don't give you a break," Lewis remarks, as we talk about his daily routine. "I'll be on the side of the road issuing a citation or helping a driver, and some (not all) cars and trucks will stay in the right lane to see how close they can get to me. Some of the truck drivers will see if they can knock my hat off from the wind gusts they create. I'll hear them laughing on their CB's talking about it. It's a game to them. The left lane will be completely clear, but they won't get over."

"I train many of our new troopers. We train them to face the oncoming traffic as they talk to drivers. We have to keep an eye on approaching cars. Death is only a foot or so away at all times," he continues.

0855 hrs: We begin to follow a teal colored mini-van travelling at high speed. We follow the van for about 7 miles, as it makes multiple lane changes without signaling. Sgt. Lewis sets his cruise control. "This driver is averaging between 80 and 85 mph," he says, as he thinks out loud. "I've set the cruise control at 80 mph and the van is pulling away from us." He pulls the van over and carefully approaches the driver.

The sergeant returns to the patrol car and comments on the stop. "Looks like a family on vacation. He wasn't tailgating or cutting people off, so I'm just going to give this guy a speeding ticket. He's being civil about it." He issues the ticket and we are quickly back on the road.

"In the State of Illinois, if we issue you multiple tickets, such as a speeding ticket and an improper lane usage ticket, you can't pay the fine out of court. You have to appear in court to answer the charges. If you are from out of state, you still have to come back here and appear in court," he says.

1003 hrs: Sgt. Lewis spots a blue van ahead making multiple lane changes without signaling. We follow the van for a few miles, clocking it at 70 mph in a 55 mph speed zone. He pulls the van over and issues a speeding ticket.

1015 hrs: A young man in a red Chevy Cavalier whips around us like we're sitting still. Sgt. Lewis guns the Monte Carlo's six-banger motor as he tries to catch up to the Cavalier before it crosses into Missouri over the Martin Luther King Bridge. *(The need for the new eight-cylinder, police-equipped Camaros and Mustangs, which will arrive soon, is obvious).* "You can see how hard it is for us to go from a standstill to 80 plus mph in this car. We'll be much more effective when the new cars arrive."

Sgt. Lewis catches up to the driver in plenty of time and decides to pull him over quickly before he injures someone. The Cavalier is traveling over 80 mph, and weaving in and out of traffic on the sharp curves leading to the bridge. Although this driver had plenty of time and room to pull over before getting to the bridge, he speeds up instead. "He sees us, but he's not going to stop," quips the Sgt.

Suddenly, the Cavalier driver decides to stop on the *bridge*. With cars approaching behind us, Sgt. Lewis grabs his hat, opens his door and firmly orders the driver to "*Get off the bridge!*" The Cavalier peels out and we follow it into Missouri. Sgt. Lewis pulls the car over in a safe location and writes the ticket. He also schools the 20-year-old, not only on his driving, but also on how to safely respond to a trooper's commands to pull over.

He gets back into the patrol car and takes a deep breath. "Like I said, it gets dangerous out here. I think he thought that once he crossed the bridge, he was safe from a ticket in Missouri. We won't normally pursue a speeder into Missouri, but we commonly work both ends of the bridges. Missouri law enforcement agencies do the same thing. If a custodial arrest is necessary, we call for a Missouri car to help," said the Sergeant. I mention to him that it seems like he does as much "educating" of drivers every day as he does anything else. "Yea, I guess that's true. I suppose you could call this last one a *teachable moment*. I'm not above giving a sermon or two," he later muses. "It's part of the job."

1104 hrs: A semi-tractor trailer rig ahead is traveling at a high rate of speed. A second rig is following close behind. After a short distance, the rig begins to weave in and out of traffic, the trailer whipping and fish-tailing slightly.

We pass the first semi unnoticed, and creep a little closer to the erratic leading truck driver ahead. As he continues to change lanes rapidly, the trailer rocks precariously left and right. Now, this semi is right on the bumper of a small white car ahead of him, not more than six to ten feet, in my estimation. I talk out-loud to Sgt. Lewis, as I have a better view of how close the semi is to the car in front. "My God," I mumble, he's right on that little car's bumper. He can't be more than 5 or 10 feet from them." (Remember, this truck is traveling at 80-plus mph in a 65 mph zone).

"We're going to pull this guy over now, before he hurts somebody," Sgt. Lewis comments as he reaches for the light switches and calls the stop in to headquarters. "This is the kind of driver who kills people," he continues. (I agree whole heartedly). After we travel at least two miles trying to get the trucker to pull over, the new, shiny rig finally comes to a stop on the right shoulder.

I watch as the driver comes to the back of the truck with his paperwork and begins talking with Sgt. Lewis. *I roll down the passenger side window and strain to hear their conversation. The road traffic noise is very heavy, making it hard to hear.*

However, Sgt. Lewis's mannerisms and body language and that of the driver tell me a lot as I observe the exchange. This driver is very friendly, cooperative, and affable. In fact, he is somewhat goofy, as he laughs and smiles through the whole ordeal:

Sgt. Lewis: "Do you know how fast you were going?"

Driver: "Yup, 82." (With a big grin.)

Sgt. Lewis: "How long have you been driving?"

Driver: (Grinning bigger now) "Well, this is my first day."

Sgt. Lewis: "Are you telling me that this is your first day driving this truck, and you're speeding, tailgating, and weaving like that?"

Driver: (Now displaying a full Jimmy Carter smile.)

"Well, I've been driving a long time. *I just took a year off to let my license clear up.* This is my first run in a year....."

Sgt. Lewis returns to the patrol car to write up the ticket after telling the driver to complete his logbook, which is a little behind. "I expected this guy to have an attitude, but he doesn't. In fact, he is smiling through the whole thing. He's so goofy, it's hard to get upset at him," Sgt. Lewis says in disbelief.

"There are some very good truck drivers out here," the sergeant comments. "But guys like this one are scary. It's drivers like this guy who give truckers a bad name," he continues. "Yeah," I respond. "I can't believe someone this goofy is driving up to 80,000 pounds down the highway. This is a little scary."

Once the paperwork is completed, the trucker is free to continue on his way. As an observer, I worry to myself about the next 1,000 plus miles he will travel as he makes his way to his destination, Rhode Island. Will he kill somebody before he gets there, or will this ticket be a lesson to him? Something tells me that he'll just laugh it off and keep on barreling recklessly along.

I also feel for the decent, hard working truck drivers out there who have to put up with drivers like this guy among their ranks. Just like all of us, truckers, the backbone of our economy, need self-esteem, too. Guys like this one ought to be doing something for a living that is a little less dangerous to themselves and the public. I'm not exaggerating here: this driver acted like Pee Wee Herman on Prozac.....wow, this was definitely the prize stop of the morning!

1127 hrs: We make one more stop, a woman in a

Suzuki Esteem, with a handicapped license plate. We followed her for several miles as she traveled at between 80 and 85 mph in a 65 mph zone while making abrupt lane changes without signaling.

As Sgt. Lewis returns to the car, he says that this lady, "Says that she didn't know how fast she was going." I smile to myself and wonder out loud. "Someone is traveling between 80 to 85 mph and has no idea how fast they're going? Wow, that's a little scary." Sgt. Lewis looks up from under the stiff brim of his trooper's hat with a slight grin: "I think she knew."

A Layman's Analysis

Whether you drive a car, a pickup truck, a semi, or some other vehicle in the state of Illinois, you best obey the traffic laws. (Myself included.) As a layman, observing the Road Rage Aggressive Driver Detail first hand, I'm glad these troopers and others like them are out there. As a family man with a wife and six kids, I have plenty to worry about when they venture onto our roads and highways.

"We want people to know that if you are going to drive in our state, you are very welcome, " said M/Sgt. Stokes. "However, as a driver on our roads, you will behave yourself and obey our laws, or you will stand a good chance of being caught: and once caught, you will pay heavy fines. We want everyone to know that we are very fair, but also very firm. It is our job to protect, serve, and save lives. We will simply not put up with dangerous drivers in Illinois."

What I observed during my ride with Sgt. Lewis, bears out the comments made by M/Sgt. Stokes. We tailed all of these drivers for at least several miles before pulling them over. "I want to make sure that the driver is intentionally driving that way, and not just passing or having a moment of inattention, or something," said Sgt. Lewis during the ride.

In this author's view, that's fair enough. In each case, there was no doubt that the driver was speeding, and in most cases, driving dangerously as well.

There is another aspect of my observations that morning that few of us outside of law enforcement ever get the opportunity to see, or much less think or care about: *These dedicated men and women are risking their lives every day out there on our highways.*

During the ride that morning, Sgt. Lewis was constantly watching traffic passing by only inches away. He was trying not to get run over while at the same time being ever watchful of the driver he had just pulled over. Will the next car produce a gun wielding maniac? A trooper never knows.

"I once stopped a suspect who had just beat up his girlfriend and her 70-year-old grandmother. He was a very big man. After a short car chase, he pulled over. I spoke to him for a few minutes and returned to my car to process him. It seemed like he was calming down and willing to cooperate, when all of a sudden, he turned around and charged my patrol car," Sgt. Lewis explained. "He jumped on the hood, caving it in, then smashed out my windshield. Next, he jumped on the roof and started smashing it in. When I opened my car door and started to get out, he jumped on me. We wrestled for maybe three or four minutes as he tried continuously to get my gun out of its holster. This really was a serious fight. I had to hit that guy at least fifteen times before his knees buckled. All I could do then was push him to the ground and hold him there as he continued to try for my gun. I was so exhausted I couldn't even lift my arms to cuff him. Luckily, I soon saw other troopers coming to my aid. If you don't think that three minutes is a very long time, try fighting that long. *Believe me, when you're fighting for your life, it's a long time!"*

Between the passing drivers who refuse to give these officers an inch and the possible lethal danger that could await them in any vehicle they pull over, they really do have their hands full. I walked away with a deeper appreciation and respect for troopers and traffic law personnel everywhere, and the dangers they face everyday. *These professionals really do care about our safety.*

Will this special unit and others like it across the nation make a difference in the long run? This author hopes they do. So well disguised are these cars that Sgt. Lewis has had one rookie trooper pull over twice thinking he was a stranded motorist as he was conducting stationary patrol on the interstate shoulder. "At least I know he's doing his job," the sergeant laughed.

One thing is for sure: there are five drivers who will remember the morning of June 30, 1998, for some time to come. The day when a sporty Monte Carlo piloted by a trooper in a Smokey-the-Bear hat pulled them over.

Until drivers everywhere start changing their attitudes about driving safety, Stokes, Sergeant Lewis, and others like them across the nation will keep educating aggressive drivers one at a time. Stokes put the issue into clear focus: "There will always be vehicle crashes caused by a number of factors. What we are trying to do is stop the needless deaths out here. We have families, too, and we worry about them when they drive. There are just too many people dying needlessly and senselessly on our roads. We are doing everything we can to help stop it."

Gene P. Martin, the new Illinois State Police Director, and a 37 year veteran of the ISP, is an ardent supporter of the Road Rage Aggressive Driver Detail. In one of his very first acts in office, he pushed the order for the new covert patrol cars through governmental red tape, expediting their delivery. A few weeks after my ride with Sgt. Lewis, the unit received two brand new covert patrol cars: a black 1998 Chevy Camaro and a white Ford Mustang. It appears that the special detail is here to stay.

As we say our good-byes in the headquarters lobby and I head for the door, I glance up one more time at a display case mounted on the wall. Inside, are the badges of Illinois State Troopers who were killed in the line of duty. It is a silent memorial to their sacrifice.

I drive away watching my speed *carefully* as I head back to Missouri. Say, is that a black sports car behind me?

Never Give an Inch

Across the U.S., troopers, sheriff's deputies, police, and pedestrians are being run over on the side of the road at an alarming rate. One recent report stated that some 3,000 people die each year as they change tires, change drivers, or in the case of law enforcement, fire, rescue, and ambulance personnel, assist injured motorists or stop them for traffic related offenses.

Although some readers might ask what these types of accidents have to do with road rage-type behavior, I would argue that such behavior is indicative of the kind of *who-gives-a-damn* attitude so many drivers display nowadays on our roadways. Just as Sgt. Troy Lewis described earlier. Today, there are those who never give an inch to anyone on the road, whether traveling next to them or if they're on the side of the road. The closer the close call, the better. Many even think it's funny.

Four Troopers Run Over in Indiana

In Indiana, the state legislature has gotten serious about this type of deadly behavior. At the time of this writing, four troopers have been killed on Indiana's roads in the last four years, two in the last year alone, as they were performing their job along a roadside. The latest death was that of Trooper Richard Gaston, who was run down by a tractor-trailer rig on the Indiana Toll Road.[41]

Two years ago, Master Trooper Andrew Winzenread stopped to help a motorist on I-74 near Greensburg when a truck veered off the road and killed him. His daughter was just one month old when he was killed. Master Trooper David Deuter died in 1998 when he was run over along the side of the road. Though seriously injured when he was struck by a car in March, Trooper Dan Hearon, was able to attend the signing ceremony for a new law.

The Indiana State Legislature has just passed a new, stricter law which increases punishment for those who fail to slow down or if possible, change lanes when they are approaching a stopped ambulance, police car, or fire truck. The new law is an attempt to stem the carnage, which is mounting from such driver indifference. Indiana Governor Frank O'Bannon signed the law on April 19, 1999.

Chapter Fourteen

The Pressures of Today

There are a number of different theories on the causes of road rage. Depending on the expert you talk to, road rage behavior is caused by everything from bad roads, congestion, and too many cars, to a decline of moral responsibility and caring for our fellow man around the world. Few drivers, including this author, would deny that these and other generalizations of road and driving related issues are a real part of the problem. However, discussing them does little toward beginning to solve the problem unless we gain a deeper insight into the details of these issues.

In this chapter, we look at some of these details and focus on the stress filled everyday life of today's drivers. These are the same pressures they face daily when they crawl behind the wheel.

If we are ever going to make a dent in driver attitudes, we must first take a practical look at the causes and effects, the daily frustrations. What is actually going on in their lives that can cause them to erupt on the road? Most researchers agree that many of the aggressive and sometimes violent acts that occur on our roads today are often a manifestation of other serious issues going on in people's lives. They cannot seem to control, or at least handle these pressures in a rational manner.

When these pressures erupt in a person behind the wheel of a vehicle hurtling down the roadway, the results can be terrifying and tragic.

Many Factors

Experts in the field of traffic management and psychology across the nation and in other countries have for years studied the phenomenon of roadway violence. It seems there are as many explanations offered for the problem as there are experts.

Studies show that women are increasingly becoming more and more involved in road rage-type incidents. They show that the typical profile of the road rage driver is aged 16 through 26, and is male. Still other studies show that where there are more congestion and people, there is more violence. All of these studies make sense and are not hard to understand.

The individual causes of road rage are varied and many. However, there are extremes in terms of both studies and proposed solutions that should cause one to stop and take a moment to think the issues through.

For example, in terms of finding solutions, there are groups who are fighting the construction of any new roads. Some protestors are lying down across roadways in England and elsewhere.

One lady I heard on KMOX radio here in St. Louis, was so concerned about the EPA's bashing of St. Louis over missing an ozone target that she was against any new roads or improvement (widening) of existing roads. In her reasoning, if you don't build the roads, then there will be fewer cars. How is that? Will people stop having children? Will new homes not be built as well? What about highway safety? How will thousands of vehicles sitting in traffic burning fuel longer and less efficiently than at higher speeds help the ozone cause? Ridiculous, if you ask me.

Then there are those who are at the other end of the spectrum. In their minds, road rage is not a problem.

Of curious note here, I noticed during my research for this book, people who lived close to work or take mass transit don't think road rage is any worse than it has ever been. Makes sense to me - they don't drive much!

There are many proposed causes and solutions to the problem of road rage. We all have our opinions, and therefore, like everyone else involved with this emotional issue, I can only repeat what a few experts are saying and offer my own opinions. One thing is for sure: nearly everyone I spoke with about the subject was polarized in their opinions on the matter.

A Deluge of Cell Phone Calls

Sergeant Strachota of the Milwaukee Sheriff's Department, was kind enough to give us his opinion as to the causes of road rage as well as describe how his department's road rage program is being perceived by the public.

When I asked him how the public has reacted to the departments unmarked Chevys, he said, "In the beginning, we had a good deal of opposition from some drivers. But now, I'm being deluged with cell phone calls from drivers reporting close calls and incidents with other drivers. It's taking a lot of my time to follow up on the calls, but I think it's worth it," he said.

"For example, one lady called me half scared to death. Here in Milwaukee, we have small red lights at some of our on ramps. These lights help us control congestion by metering vehicles onto the highway.

"The woman said that a man had become angry with her for some altercation, and moments later he was stopped by the onramp metering light with her directly behind him. Apparently, he had gotten out of his car and approached her. When he reached her car, he began screaming at her, foul language and all. With three or four cars behind her blocking her in, she had no way to escape the man. Although he didn't physically attack her, she had no way of knowing if he was going to at any minute or had a weapon with him. After the light changed, he was still there screaming at her."

Making House Calls

"When it was over, she called me on her cell phone and gave me the license number. When I called him, he was at first arrogant, but then calmed down as we talked. Like many of the violators I talk to on the phone, they get very upset when I refer to them as a participant in road rage. They don't see themselves as *bad* or *aggressive* people. But like most I've talked to, this guy soon admitted that he had displayed rage toward the woman and had probably scared her to death."

The Sergeant went on to say that he's not sure how much of an impact his small, unique patrol is making on the problem of aggressive driving, and in particular, road rage, but like all things, it will take time to see the results. "As we continue to get the word out and people see us in action, we hope to make a difference. Judging from the phone calls we're getting, the public, apprehensive at first, is now beginning not only to accept the idea, but is seeking us out for help. That's what we're here for."

When I asked him what the legal issues are surrounding such a verbal attack, Sgt. Strachota said that in the screaming incident, for example, the woman could have pressed charges. "If she had wanted to press charges, I would have taken them both before the District Attorney. It would have been his decision as to how to proceed. Most people just want me to set the aggressor straight and put a little fear into them about what they've done. A few drivers admit they've got a problem and say they're going to change their ways. They say they 'just didn't realize how they had been driving.'"

Tailgating -
The Most Prevalent Cause of Problems

"From what we've seen, I believe that tailgating is the most prevalent cause of serious accidents, regardless of speed, and it causes a lot of anger on the road as well," said the Sergeant. "I believe, from the reaction most people have, that many of them just don't realize how their driving habits have changed. They especially don't seem to realize how bad they've become at tailgating. It seems that everyone is doing it, so they just go along with the crowd."

Few drivers could argue with Sgt. Strachota's observations on tailgating. As we've mentioned elsewhere, some veteran officers are beginning to believe that the new sophisticated anti-locking braking systems on today's cars are giving people a dangerous sense of always being able to stop in time.

Although modern braking systems are much improved over older systems, variables such as wet roads, varying driver reaction times, distractions, etc., can't be controlled by the driver. Relying on your brake to stop in time while tailgating is a real bad idea.

Losing Your Head - Literally

"Of all the things that can happen to you out there as a driver," continued the Sergeant, "I've now become paranoid of flying debris. Whether I'm in a patrol car or my personal car, several deadly encounters with cars and debris around Milwaukee have caused me to back off even farther from the vehicles ahead of me than ever."

"One poor guy was following another car when the car ahead dislodged a 75 pound steel plate and flipped it upright. Because he was following so close, the plate went through his windshield. *It went through his face and out the back window, barely slowing down,"* he said.

Sergeant Strachota continued, "In another accident, a piece of metal fell off of a truck ahead of a family traveling in a van. When the van drove over the metal, it went through the gas tank and punched through the bottom of the van as well. All six of the children were trapped and died in the flames.

"Flying truck springs are another deadly hazard out there," he continued. "In two separate incidents, both related to trucks losing a suspension spring, one driver had a spring go through his neck and the other his head. They never had a chance. I don't mind telling you that I've become somewhat paranoid of flying debris on the highway. When you see enough of these types of devastating accidents, you become all too aware of what can happen to you."

Author's note: Just a few weeks after speaking with Sgt. Strachota, this author was southbound on Highway 270, which skirts the outer limits of St. Louis. Just as I passed the Hwy. 44 Interchange, I saw cars scattering in all directions ahead and flashing brake lights as drivers were obviously trying to avoid something. As I drew nearer to the scene, I saw metal debris on the roadway and cars with multiple flat tires on the side of the road as people were getting out of their cars to inspect the damage.

Ironically, similar to the van fire story Sgt. Strachota had told, just ahead of me, I saw what looked like water coming from the vehicle ahead. It had obviously hit something too. As I continued to slow down and watched the car pull over,

I smelled gasoline. The driver and several other passengers got out fast. Luckily, there was no fire.

Just ahead of all the debris, was a semi sitting on the shoulder. Obviously, it had lost part of its load. The truck driver was waving his arms frantically for people to slow down.

A Rock and Roll Load

Just a few months later in August, I found myself behind a flatbed semi-tractor rig that was hauling a load of landscape rock. One of the pallets, which was on the rear of the truck, was stacked high with semi-flat rocks. There was no cage or wire around the rocks to hold them in place: only two small tie-down straps. As the truck changed lanes, the stack of rocks rocked wildly to the left, almost falling off the truck. It was obvious that the tie-down straps had become loose and it was imminent that the load was soon to fall.

Luckily, I had a CB in my pickup and I was able to contact the driver to let him know what was going on. To his credit, he quickly pulled over to re-secure the load. This was a serious close call.

This author has a renewed appreciation for trucks, and another reason not to follow them too closely!

The Passing Lane?

Sergeant Strachota made another interesting observation that no one else had mentioned to me during my research:

"Many people get upset because drivers are, in their minds, hanging out in the *fast lane*, which in most cases, is really the *passing lane*. Historically, it has been true that the left lane is only supposed to be used to pass. We also get people calling who are upset that we don't make trucks stay out of the left lane," said the Sergeant.

"On the open road, the left lane is still the passing lane. However, in Milwaukee and other cities, many of our exits and directional traffic lanes at intersections, are in the left lane. Therefore, it's neither reasonable nor possible to require slower vehicles to stay in the right, or slow lanes."

By design, we have made it necessary for vehicles of all sizes and drivers of varying skill levels, to share the same lanes. In most cases, this also means the left lanes. As Sergeant Strachota points out, this can be a recipe for disaster, even for a deputy in an unmarked car going eight miles over the speed limit. In the fast lane, it can provoke an attack.

Take Me Out to the Ball Game

In a last comment from Sergeant Strachota, in an effort on his part to figure out what has been happening to our nation's drivers, he gave a 'ball park' comparison.

"I'm not sure what's been happening to our drivers up here in Milwaukee, but I can give you a good comparison," he said. "I've been working the ball park downtown for years, and let me tell you, it used to be *'hell duty.'* But over the last few years, it hasn't been bad at all. In fact, I enjoy it now. People are much more courteous. I guess you could say, that they are truly 'kinder and gentler' than they used to be."

"But put these same people behind the wheel of a car, and you have a real-life Jekyl and Hyde transformation taking place. They come from all walks of life and every age. It's truly an amazing thing to see. I sure hope we can figure it out some day. For now, all we can do is try to educate people," he concluded.

So if you ever find yourself traveling through the great town of Milwaukee, driver beware: and behave. That Chevy Lumina or Ford Escort, Corvette or mini-van in front of you could be driven by a deputy sheriff looking for trouble makers.

And you never know, you might even get arrested by a deputy in a produce truck!

The Baby Sitter

The baby sitter. Now here is an issue that most parents of the late twentieth century can relate too, especially mothers. Finding and keeping a good baby sitter can be a very difficult and frustrating experience. The task is sometimes easier if money is no object, but for most of us, there is a need to find the best and safest child care for the lowest possible cost. Many single parents must pay a small fortune for good child care, often spending a large portion of their weekly income in the process.

Unlike the fifties and sixties, today, most women must work outside the home to make ends meet. Facts and figures abound about the record number of working mothers today. Many of these mothers and fathers are single parents who must work odd shifts, which makes child care issues even tougher. Commercial child care facilities have sprung up everywhere in answer to the cry for help. But they aren't cheap, especially if you are late in picking up your child.

Married or single, the demands on our time as parents are tremendous, especially when it comes to the time it takes to drop off the kid(s) and pick them up.

What does all this have to do with road rage? Well, among other things, many commercial and some private child care facilities, do not open early enough for many commuters.

As a result, the time between when the child can be dropped off and when the parent must report to his or her job can be too tight to allow for a leisurely commute. Add to that a grumpy, unforgiving boss, and you have a recipe for trouble on the road.

The parent is caught between the demands of the child care provider and their employer. If the child care facility is late in opening up in the morning, lookout. You not only have an angry parent, but an upset commuter as well.

Such difficulties can lead to traffic confrontations due to speeding, honking, rapid lane changes, etc., on the part of the parent-employee as they struggle to make it to work on time. If this scenario happens often enough, the parent follows a typical "learned response" curve and a habit forms out of simple familiarity with the rushed routine.

The parent-employee may have done everything right: they got out of bed early, got out of the house, etc. Yet, due to circumstances beyond their control, such as an accident, they find themselves in a mad rush to get to work on time.

Five-Dollars-a-Minute Late Charge

There is another pressure that comes upon the parent-commuter on the return trip home from work: severe late charges are often levied against parents for picking up their children late from the childcare provider.

My family and I live in a bedroom community about 20 miles south of St. Louis. As such, most of the people who live in the county commute to jobs in St. Louis every day, just as millions like them do in any typical North American city or suburb.

Before and during my research for this book, I would see drivers, especially women, speeding and driving recklessly on southbound Highway 55 near my home as they made their way back into the suburbs. I would be traveling at around 75 mph in a 70 mph zone, and these drivers, again mainly women, would fly past me like I was sitting still. I couldn't help but ask myself: "Where are all these crazy women off to in such a mad rush? I'm in a hurry too, but my goodness, they're almost home. Don't they want to get there alive?"

Then one day, I read something concerning childcare providers in another U.S. city which went off like a bell in my head. The article described the severe penalties imposed on parents by child-care facilities in that city if they were late picking up their kids.

When I mentioned the story to my wife, she reacted matter-of-factly: "Oh yes, you didn't know that? Around here it's 6:00. If you don't pick up your child by 6:00, there's a $5 per minute charge for every minute you're late!"

I was flabbergasted. I then realized that most of the time, I was on that stretch of highway between 5:30 and 6:00 pm, and that many of these crazed, madly focused, speeding and weaving mothers, were trying to beat the clock to the sitter. *Five dollars a minute means that being just ten minutes late will cost you $50!* God forbid if an accident delays you for say, 30 minutes. Now the penalty goes up to $150! For many parents, especially single moms, this is a hit in the pocket book they simply can't afford. Being just one hour late, can wipe out a week's take home pay. While it is understandable that many child care providers have enacted such a rule to keep parents from abusing them by things such as shopping trips to the grocery store on the way home, thus eating into the provider's own free time, it seems as though these penalties are severe. To top that off, many childcare facilities are all booked up too, and many have waiting lists. Tick off the sitter, and look out. You may not be able to go to work tomorrow for lack of some place safe to leave your child.

It would seem as though some child care providers have found both a valuable commodity in our latchkey kids and a convenient source of revenue over and above what would seem reasonable. Sort of a new "gold rush" in some cases. In other forms of business, such fleecing of an adult is tantamount to extortion.

Employers and Child Care Providers Can Help

On our nation's highways, the result of such pressure on parent-commuters by some employers and childcare providers can, and often does, lead to aggressive driving and sometimes road rage. Employers can help by using flex-time and telecommuting where possible, and by encouraging their supervisors to bend a sympathetic ear toward employees who are experiencing such problems. Employees who become obvious abusers of the situation can be dealt with accordingly.

Some companies have gone to in-house childcare facilities. For companies that can afford such a solution, it would seem that their parent/employees would find the in-house solution to be a godsend.

Childcare providers can help by being more reasonable in the financial demands they levy on parents for being a few minutes late. Even if a late charge is used, and in some cases, necessary, they can at least be more reasonable in the amounts charged. *(One of my daughters has worked as a child care provider for years, so I know that some people do abuse the rules, making it tough on the provider's employees, who have lives too, and the other parent-commuters).* Some childcare providers only charge about a dollar per minute, which although still steep, is much more reasonable than five dollars per minute.

Unknowingly, some employers and childcare providers are contributing to the rise in tension on our roadways, which often results in speeding, road rage and sometimes death, by creating unnecessary time related stress on their employees and customers. If you are an employer or childcare provider, you can help reduce stress on our roads. Please take time to examine your policies and work practices. As an employer, you just might prevent a crippling injury or death of an employee by giving them a break.

As a childcare provider, by becoming more understanding and reasonable, you'll be helping to ensure that the little boy or girl in your care still has a mom or dad to pick them up: that they are not orphaned at the end of the day. Is a few extra bucks worth a life?

The Foreign Driver

A Passage from India

One of the aspects of road rage I wanted to explore for this book was the element of the "foreign driver." This is no doubt a controversial subject, and in no way is it intended to be racist or ethnophobic in nature, but only an observation this author has made from personal experience. I bring it up here only to illustrate the many cultural differences that can effect our safety on the highways.

As a construction and operations manager for a large Department of Energy Superfund cleanup site, I have had the opportunity to meet and work with a number of people from many other countries as well as from all over the United States.

Several years ago, we had a rash of auto accidents on the construction site which spurred my curiosity. The main thing that caught my eye was that although we only had four men from India on site, three of the four had been involved in accidents while driving government vehicles on site. The fourth man had wrecked his personal car on several occasions, and the other three seemed to have had problems away from work as well.

I do not mention the following drivers from India to pick on that culture, but rather to help us gain a better understanding of foreign drivers in general and the difficulties they face on the road. And to explore how their driving can effect the rest of us.

Bicycle Rider Body-Slams a Parked Pickup Truck Broadside

On one occasion, a large, likable, and friendly gentleman from India was riding a balloon tired bicycle when he ran the bike into the side of a pickup truck at a fairly high rate of speed.

At somewhere in the 300 pound range, his large body reportedly slammed into the side of the parked truck with a great deal of force. The resulting sound effect reportedly resembled that of a lightning strike. The impact was enough to cause well over two thousand dollars worth of damage.

To our amazement, the bicyclist stood up, dusted himself off, and grinned, embarrassed, at the few witnesses to the bizarre wreck. It's not every day that a bicyclist's body slams a full grown pickup truck in such a manner, especially in a wide open area. When questioned, he said that he had just lost control. Wow! Hulk Hogan, move over!

Golf Cart Attacks Pickup

In another incident, another gentleman from India, a skinny, shy, and very affable character, ran an *electric golf cart* into the side of another pickup truck. He said he thought that the brakes had not worked right, but during the accident investigation, we found them to be in good working order.

There were a few other close calls with driving company cars and pickup trucks involving a few of these Indian men that also caught my attention. On more than one occasion, I had been severely tailgated by several of them on the local roads as I came to work or as I was leaving. We had a number of other employees of Indian descent that also worked at the project, all of whom seemed to have the same aggravating, dangerous driving habits.

One day, I asked one of them, a friend of mine named Raj Ganapathy, about their driving habits. I think it went something like: "Do you people from India take any driving classes? Do they teach you how to drive over there?" In answer to my question, Raj laughed loudly. "Not really," he responded.

Raj and I worked together for over six years. He was born and raised in a city called Madras, in southeast India, a town with nearly *15 million residents.*

"Let me put it to you this way," Raj said. "There are well over 14 million people in my home town. To serve them, there are only, let's say, about 10 driver's license offices, each with a small staff. Do you think 10 offices can properly license hundreds of thousands of drivers?" he continued.

"When I went to get my driver's license, the line was huge, as it always is. There were at least 400 to 500 people waiting to take the test. It's common to stand there all day and never get a chance to take the test," Raj commented. "I was standing there in line for a while when an official approached me and said: 'Do you want to stand in this line all day, or would you like to pay me 10 bucks and you can have your license now?' Of course, I paid him the 10 bucks and left with my license. From that day on, I was a licensed driver."

Raj went on to describe driving in his home town: "People in America get all upset about 40,000 people or more killed in this country every year. *In my home town alone, more than 10,000 people die every year.* While I was growing up, I must have seen at least 15 people die right in front of me. Things are much different in India. When a car comes sailing down the road, you had better get out of the way. The roads are often choked with people and animals, and drivers are always running over them. In India, red means stop, green means go, *and amber or yellow, means do whatever you want.*"

As our conversation continued, Raj went on to talk about coming to America and driving here. "I bought an international driver's license before I came here. When you buy an international license, you obviously keep the license from your country of origin, which in my case, is India. Should anyone with an international license have their license revoked, they still have their original license to drive on. If need be, they just go get another international license and keep right on going," Raj said.

"When I got here, everything was different. The steering wheels were on the other side of the car, people here drive on the opposite side of the road than we do in India, all the road signs were different, and so on. Basically, almost everything about driving here in America was different, including driving manners. In India, driving manners don't really exist. It's every man for himself."

Toward the end of our conversation, Raj told me that after he nearly caused a wreck or two, he found someone here to give him some driving lessons. "I was driving terribly," he admitted. "I wanted to do the right thing, so I got some help."

"I thought I was a good driver, but my wife and mother-in-law were always on my back and said I was terrible behind the wheel. I drove them crazy with my erratic driving. I finally realized that I needed help. Now, I'm glad I got some."

The Melting Pot

As the above driving stories reflect, the United States is still the world's melting pot. And, there is no place in the

U.S. where that melting pot is more visible, and at times, more dangerous, than on our roads.

Let's think about this subject for a minute. Who is out there on the roads with us? Where did they come from? What are our varying political, social, and customs differences? How do we think differently? How do these differences possibly effect our attitudes and habits when we drive?

Well, for starters, as we've been discussing, drivers from foreign countries like Japan, Germany, Australia, India, Mexico, South America, and other points around the globe, continue to migrate in large numbers to the U.S.

So, like the Indian men we talked about above, these people of different cultures, languages, and social behavior, not only must learn a new language and way of life, but they must adapt to our driving culture as well.

What this means is that the next time you get into a driving conflict or get tailgated by a foreigner, try to remember that they might not know any better. Soon enough, they will learn, but hopefully, they'll catch on before they hurt themselves or someone else. If you know a foreigner who drives like they're captain of the Batmobile, you might try talking to them rationally about their driving skills and suggest some training for them. You might keep them alive!

The Car Culture Clash

Whether a driver is a member of the affluent society, zooming around town in a Mercedes or Porsche, or at the low end of the driving scale, puttering around in an old rust bucket, or somewhere in between, there is one place we will all come together: *the road.*

There is no escaping it. The roads in this country belong to us all: rich, poor, or of average income, white, red, black, or yellow. We all own and pay for them together.

Isolationism

One social aspect of driving in the U.S. that I have yet to see discussed in print anywhere is the issue of "cultural isolationism," and how this issue can relate to aggression on our roads. Maybe it's too controversial or politically dangerous to speak of it. Personally, I feel that it is at a minimum, a peripheral cause of road aggression, or as a minimum, serves to exacerbate road confrontations once they occur.

The wealthy, for example, have their own exclusive communities. These communities, filled with expensive homes, high-end shops and grocery stores, exclusive boutiques, etc., are usually well insulated and separated from surrounding communities.

Indeed, pressure is placed on law enforcement agencies in these elite communities to make the police detect loitering outsiders and keep them out of town. The wealthy simply demand such attention by the authorities whose salaries they pay.

Likewise, the poor live largely in regionalized community clusters, complete with poor roads, low-end stores, and generally, a more deprived environment. Interestingly, many poor people never get out of their towns, as is the case for some of the wealthy.

For the people in between, or the *middle class* (the Wal-mart and K-Mart crowds, soccer moms, etc.) there are the suburbs, where they have developed their own life style and culture. Foreigners, depending on their financial status, can fall into any one of these three main groups of people.

However, regardless of your income, status, or isolation from the outside world, there is one inescapable fact when it comes to traveling: if you are going to drive from St. Louis to Kansas City, you will be traveling on Interstate 70. Denver to Colorado Springs? You'll be on I-25. Los Angeles to San Francisco? Chances are, you'll be traveling on Highway 5.

In other words, every kind of vehicle from expensive German sports cars to rusty road bombs will be out there on the road together. And so, there will be drivers of every social and cultural background out there on the roadway together.

Therefore, somehow, we have to learn to get along together. There will be families, businessmen, working moms, cowboys, red necks, foreigners, criminals, preachers, and every sort of person you could possibly imagine on the roads with you.

Now, let's throw in the racists, bigots, hot tempered, testosterone-heavy male teens, the late-to-work moms, the wannabe race car drivers, the semi-drivers who are running late and dodging "four wheelers," as they call automobiles, construction crews, and so on, and you've got a real mess!

Longer Work Hours, Less Time Off

Over the last decade, there has been quite a change in how we as Americans are working. Numerous polls show that employers are giving fewer perks to employees nowadays. Employers have been reducing benefits, out-sourcing, hiring millions of part-timers to avoid having to provide insurance and other benefits, working employees harder and longer, and in general, doing their best to destroy any good will and company loyalty they may have generated in the past.

Today, in most companies, it's all profits and production for the company, with little regard for employee welfare. Lookout corporate America: this strategy *will* eventually backfire on you. One thing is sure: the effects of these and other pressures have already caused explosive tempers on our roads. Anyone who doesn't believe that is either in denial, is blind, or lives so far back in the hills some place that they are oblivious to today's driving realities.

The Young "Super Workers" of Today:
A Recipe for Disaster

Younger people coming into today's work force, have been convinced by those interested in maximizing productivity that they "really don't need much time off." These young hopefuls are hiring on at good wages; most are just happy to be employed; and many are starting off at fairly high salaries as compared to the generations before. What many of them probably don't realize, however, is that the major source of tension they are feeling in their lives could well be that they rarely take a break from their toil and fast-paced lives.

This author has seen many an interview on television and in print where the freshly graduated, freshly hired, bright-eyed college grad is asked about working a lot of overtime and getting little time off. "The older generation takes too much time off," is a standard response. I've heard them say things like: "I love to work; I want to be successful and surpass what my parents accomplished. Who needs a vacation?"

OK, my young friend, we'll eagerly await your opinion in 5 or 10 years when you're completely dissatisfied with your life and burned out. Trust me, you've been duped, and chances are, we may see you relieving your pent up aggression on the roadways. If this is you, stop and think about your life. Do you really think that you can work 12 hours a day, 6 or 7 days a week for the rest of your life without a break now and then?

The Japan Factor

The Japanese, if you will remember, for many years, kicked America's tail when it came to productivity. All we heard from politicians and corporate spokesmen, was how superior in workmanship and dedicated to their employers the Japanese worker was when compared with America's workforce. Mantras went out from the halls of U.S. corporations crying, "If we could only be more like our Japanese friends, we would be number one again. We've got to learn from them. This is critical to our survival as a nation. If we could only be more like the Japanese....."

Well, guess what? We've just about made it. These corporations used these comparisons to support their efforts at convincing U.S. workers to work harder, smarter, longer. "If we just work together, we can lick 'em!" I have no problem with the dramatic increase in the quality of U.S. manufactured goods. It was sorely needed. However, there is more to learn from the Japanese. Namely, just how much of a toll the rush to out-work and out-produce the world has taken on the Japanese people.

What Happened

Some 20 or so years ago, the Japanese worker had become convinced that "work is all-important: everything else is secondary." The comparisons being played out at the time in the U.S., which touted and praised the Japanese worker and roundly criticized U.S. workers as "lazy," served to pour even more fuel on the Japanese productivity fire.

The Japanese worker pushed ever harder, working longer hours, forgoing time off, giving up much of their family time for the sake of the company. Japanese companies became super-rich and profitable. Japanese banks became "lenders to the world."

However, a few years ago, that philosophy began to unravel as millions of worn-out and fed-up Japanese workers began to break down from the pressure. They began to demand time off to play golf, spend time with their families, travel, and engage in similar things that their U.S. and European counterparts were doing. They started to realize that they were not able to enjoy the fruits of their labor. That out-producing the world was not enough to sustain their desire for at least minimal leisure time. They began to demand a little time to themselves to wind down and enjoy life.

Today, as this book goes to print, their economy is in a shambles. Geared to massive production, it is reeling with bankruptcies. Next time, the Japanese worker just might be a little more guarded when their managers resurrect their productivity speeches, company-sponsored exercise classes, company parades, uniforms, and other "teaming" events. They probably won't be too quick to rush to the corporate gym to perform their morning jumping jacks. People need down time, period. You simply just can't unwind otherwise. It's a law of nature.

The U.S. Becomes Japanized

After more than 10 years of trying, U.S. employers have succeeded in skillfully increasing their productivity by using the Japanese model of excellence. Today, employees of U.S. companies are working harder for less. But afraid of losing their jobs to foreigners or younger upstarts, many don't speak up. Instead, they do as their Japanese counterparts did for several decades: they just take it and push harder. Meanwhile, they mow their grass after dark, miss the kids sports events, eat their meals alone, and put up with a host of other abnormal changes in their lives.

These changes have brought many advantages to the employer: reductions in the amount of additional employees they must hire, reductions in expensive medical coverage, corporate liability is kept to a minimum, people-related problems are kept low, etc., all of which result in higher profits for the company...and more stress for the worker.

Much of this "new strategy" is predictable. After all, much of our corporate community has been clamoring about Japanese companies for years, sending productivity specialists to Japan to learn their "secrets" of productivity. Many coveted productivity awards, such as the Malcom Baldridge Award, given out each year in the U.S. are solely Japanese-theory based.

So, what is *really* at the heart of these Japanese productivity secrets? In this author's view, it's very simple. I've lived through, and been a part of, many of these corporate strategies:

"We will work them harder, but only after we have prepared them mentally. We will use teaming concepts where they are made to feel more important by working together for a common goal (sure sounds Japanese, doesn't it?). We will set up committees, give more important titles to them, and push decisions down to the lowest levels. We will condition their minds through this training. They will learn to produce more." (And what you don't hear: "At the same time, the fear of losing their jobs, either through company moves to Mexico or elsewhere out of the country, should also help to keep them in line.")

Now, I'm not saying all of this is bad stuff. In fact, some of it is welcomed. After all, it's high time managers started listening to their workers. However, there is absolutely no substitute for a vacation, Sundays at home with family or friends, and other "my time" activities. U.S. companies will eventually discover, as have the Japanese, the lessons of bringing up a generation of workaholics. There is little doubt in my mind that much of this pent up frustration is being vented on our roads, as these overworked, glassy-eyed human go-bots, grab the wheel and speed home in an effort to enjoy what little time to themselves they are allowed. I doubt that many of you would disagree!

As for the fear factor, this has already begun to backfire on U.S. corporations as workers are now leaving these companies by the thousands. This is America, not Japan. Americans will only put up with so much malarkey before they hit the bricks.

Chapter Fifteen

Bad Roads, Bridges, and Highways
Fueling the Road Rage Phenomenon?

In this chapter, we examine the condition of our nations highway and road systems, and their potential effects on road rage and aggressive driving. A careful study of these issues is needed if we are to fully understand the growing problem of violence and aggression on our roads. Few Americans would argue that roads and bridges everywhere are in terrible shape and are in need of serious repair and upgrades. Let's take a look at what some of the country's leading researchers have to say on this important topic.

The Gasoline Tax

Most drivers are aware that when they purchase gas anywhere in the United States, they are paying a hefty sum in federal taxes at the same time. We are also paying state, and sometimes local taxes for each gallon of gas. State and local taxes vary widely across the country. However, the federal tax on gasoline is the same for everyone.

At the time of this writing, the federal gasoline tax stands at 18.4 cents per gallon. This figure equates to a huge federal intake in funds, which are mandated by law to go solely toward the repair of our roads and bridges, construction of new roads and bridges, and improvement and maintenance of our existing roadway systems. These systems include stoplights, shoulders, overpasses, intersections, guardrails, and other road and bridge related structures.[42]

However, like other government taxes, what goes into the federal till is rarely, if ever, equal to what trickles back out to the states. The federal gasoline tax is no different

TRIP - The Road Information Program

Located in the heart of our nation's capitol is a privately funded organization called "The Road Information Program," better known as **"TRIP."**

TRIP is a non-government, non-profit research group. It has been keeping tabs on highway and bridge related government spending for many years. We contacted the organization and asked them some tough questions about how our federal highway tax dollars are being spent. Their answers were to the point.

Underlying Causes of Road Anger

As we said above, the professionals at TRIP keep a close watch on U.S. Government highway spending. This nonprofit group is supported by highway and bridge construction companies and many other private organizations with concerns or interests related to the nation's highways, bridges, and other road-related systems and infrastructures.

The 'Road to Hell'

In a May 1998 news release, TRIP said that America's motorists are being forced to travel on the 'Road to Hell' as they drive on crumbling highways. In a nutshell, TRIP says that although there are huge amounts of highway and bridge dollars sitting in government accounts, the money is not being used properly, or more importantly, not at all. *(Funds were later released and many road and bridge projects funded in 1998.)*

"As many as 12,000 lives a year are lost on our nation's highways because of roadside hazards and inadequate roadway conditions," said William M. Wilkins, TRIP's Executive Director.

"As our nation's lawmakers prepare to put the final touches on the highway transportation bill, they should keep their focus on the fact that this funding will go to make safety improvements that will benefit all motorists - and all motorists are taxpayers."

Wilkins went on to say that Americans would "continue to drive the Road to Hell every day as they drive on crumbling roadways *and sit for hours in traffic. (And we all know how tempers often flair up when hot, miserable, tired drivers are stuck for hours in traffic).* He went on to say that congress needs to pass a new highway bill with 'greatly increased funding levels' to correct the problem.

In March 1998, the U.S. Senate approved a $214 billion highway bill by a 96-4 margin. On April 1, just weeks later, the Hose followed suit by approving a different $218 billion bill by a 303-80 margin.

There are those who disagree with TRIP and others concerning a new highway bill. (These bills, once approved, last four or five years, after which, a new bill must be approved and funded.) Some of these groups say there is too much "pork" in the proposed bill. *Basically, they'd like to see the money go elsewhere.* Although this author would rather stay out of the debate between these groups, *one would have to be blind to not see the decaying highway and bridge infrastructures around us.*

"Those who suggest that the bill contains too much 'pork' do not understand that the highway projects are designed to make needed safety improvements," Wilkins said. "For decades, our nation's highway transportation system has suffered from insufficient funding. This isn't about pork. It's about making improvements to save lives, reduce congestion, and repair our roads and bridges."

Indeed, the U.S. Department of Transportation, which released a detailed 1997 report on our nation's transportation needs, said congress would have to double the current level of transportation spending if we are to make the type of improvements that will benefit motorists in the twenty first century.

Wilkins pointed out that there is overwhelming support in both houses of Congress and from a broad range of public officials. According to Wilkins, groups such as the National Governors' Association, the U.S. Chamber of Commerce, the

AFL-CIO, and the American Association of State Highway and Transportation Officials, all support the legislation.

Part Three

The Keys to Highway Survival

In Part Three, we look at the ways in which drivers can avoid becoming a statistic. We also look at the many efforts that are being launched around the world to fight road rage, especially those programs being initiated across the U.S.

Federal, state, and local governments everywhere are beginning to realize that something must be done about the lethal hazards of enraged drivers. Legislators and police agencies are fighting back with stiff penalties and harsh fines, including extended jail time for proven road rage defendants.

It is my belief that in the long run, you cannot legislate morality, kindness, and goodwill among the masses. However, until the masses decide to stop the carnage on their own, governments big and small are doing whatever they can to reduce the toll.

Chapter Sixteen

Understanding the Modern Trucker

The Modern Truck Driver

It would be irresponsible of this author, if this book focused only on the "sensational," bad side of the trucking industry. This includes road rage-type truckers and the crashes they may sometimes cause, without also exploring the realities of this important industry, including highway safety. Although few would argue that the Trifon Lee Athnos road rage case is a terrifying case, as we have said, Mr. Athnos' behavior was extreme, and *is not* typical of the average 90's or Y2K truck driver.

Nuclear Missiles

From 1977 through 1981, this author was a Minuteman III Intercontinental Ballistic Missile (ICBM) Mechanic in the U.S. Air Force. One of my duties was to drive a semi-tractor, loaded with the most powerful weapons in the world, nuclear warheads. As a 21-year-old sergeant, I had a great deal of responsibility and pressure on my shoulders. From my own truck driving experiences during those early years, I know full well how stupid some drivers can behave around semi's...even those loaded with nuclear bombs.

During our convoys between F.E. Warren AFB in Cheyenne, Wyoming, and 200 remote Minuteman III Missile Sites spread out over the high plains of Colorado, Nebraska, and Wyoming, we would have an average of 13 vehicles in the convoy. Most of these vehicles were loaded with fire teams (men with grenade launchers, assault rifles, etc.). Mounted on top of these vehicles were flashing red and blue lights as we moved across Interstate Highways 25 and 80 and across two lane back roads.

Along the travel route, an armored personnel carrier with machine guns would be stationed at every overpass. High above, a Cobra Helicopter gun ship circled, looking for any sign of terrorist activity. In front of the convoy, U.S. Marshals in a Blazer would clear the road ahead as we traveled to the missile site or back to the base.

Obviously, the main concern was always the threat of a terrorist attack. All of us, including myself as the driver, wore combat helmets, flak jackets, and .38 caliber revolvers. We also had sawed-off shotguns loaded with buckshot, and M-16 rifles at the ready inside the cab. We were anti-terrorist trained and ready to defend the nuclear warhead we were transporting with our lives. (In fact, protecting the warhead with our lives was a direct order).

Incredibly, however, people driving on the highways in passenger vehicles, even upon seeing the show of military might behind them in their rearview mirror, would sometimes refuse to get out of the way. The U.S. Marshals would have to pull them over to get them out of our way so the convoy could pass.

On a few occasions, a driver would try and cut in front of the semi I was driving, which was hauling the nuclear warhead. You can imagine the mayhem that followed! We never knew if it might be a terrorist trying to pull something or not. The convoy would instantly come to life, and shortly thereafter, the driver of that vehicle would be wishing he never hesitated to get out of the way.

Add bad weather and slick roads to the mix, and look out, you could really have a circus on your hands! Today's semi's are larger, heavier, and more powerful than ever before. Having driven a semi carrying the most powerful weapons on earth, I can tell you that automobile drivers pull some incredibly stupid acts around these big rigs. Truckers spend a good deal of their driving time dodging cars, pickups, and other vehicles as they whip in and out of traffic lanes in front and behind them.

Sharing the Road

Now let us move on to the main point in this chapter: The big rigs are here to stay and we have to learn to share the road with them.

If we are ever to make our highways safer and friendlier, it is vital that we begin to understand the other road users out there on the highways with us.

The last statement is true for all drivers, motorcyclists, cyclists, pedestrians, etc. There will never be, and cannot be, change without first coming to a better understanding of our fellow travelers. Of all the drivers who are misinterpreted, misunderstood, and most often criticized these days, the truck driver is tops.

Although some truck drivers are dangerous, just as other types of drivers can be, it isn't fair to label all truckers together as "road hogs" or as being dangerous.

"The trucking industry has not always done a good job in telling its story, and we'd like to help correct that," says George Estok, President of John Deere Transportation Insurance, which insures semi-tractor-trailer operators. "As one of the nation's largest insurers of owner-operator and small-to-mid-sized fleets, we at John Deere Transportation Insurance are concerned that the rancor and misunderstanding between truckers, shippers, and the motoring public threaten our transportation system and the lives of our nation's motorists," he continues.[43]

Dramatic Increases in Trucking Activity

Trucking is a *huge* business. *Today, there are over 3 million truck divers on U.S. roads.* In addition, there are 7.9 million non-driver related trucking jobs. In the state of Illinois, for example, 1 out of 11 jobs is directly related to the trucking industry. Since 1960, trucking in the U.S. has increased 11 fold. In 1994, trucking represented $176.8 billion worth of business annually. [44]

So, suffice it to say, with over 10 million workers and billions in revenue, the U.S. trucking industry is a huge part of our economy. We receive almost everything we consume by truck: hair dryers, furniture, building materials, food, fuel, clothes, toys, television sets, automobiles, and on and on.

But our main focus here is the truck drivers themselves. What stresses are they under? Don't they all make big money? Aren't they all displaced cowboys with bad attitudes? Let's examine the facts.

Accident Statistics

On the positive side of the picture, despite a huge increase in the number of trucks on the road today and total miles traveled by these big rigs, accidents per miles driven has actually been declining for a number of years. That is, until recently.

In 1985, 4,513 people died in semi-tractor-trailer related crashes. The trend continued downhill until 1992, when a total of 3,232 people died as a result of semi-tractor-trailer related crashes. In the following year, 1993, 3,469 people were killed. In 1994, the death toll increased to 3,626. The 1995 death toll was 3,576.

Why the recent increase? Although experts may disagree on some of the issues involved, the fact that semi-tractor-trailer miles driven rose from 68.6 billion in 1980 to 115 billion in 1995 obviously has something to do with it.

During this period of a booming economy, commerce increased dramatically. This robust economy required the trucking industry to nearly double in size over the same period. Although there has been a slight increase in fatalities over the last few years, it is still notable that although trucking miles nearly doubled from 1980 through 1995, the number of fatalities continued to drop. So, any way you slice it, there are proportionately fewer car/truck accidents on the basis of total truck miles driven.

Getting Out of the Way

On the cynical side, there are automobile drivers I ran across during my investigation who believe that much of the credit for this decrease goes not to the truck driver, but to other drivers who are getting out of their way. Comments such as:

"Some truckers get right on your rear bumper, even at 75 miles per hour or more. You have to get out of their way, or they'll run right over you. You know that if you had to stop suddenly, you wouldn't have a chance. You would be dead in an instant. So, you just get out of their way as fast as you can when you see them charging at you in your rearview mirror."

Fair enough. Some truckers do drive recklessly, just as other drivers do. And personally, I get out of their way, too. There are a lot of hills in my home state of Missouri, which causes many truckers to "floor it" when traveling downhill in an effort to make it up the next hill without having to dog it. If you're in their way, some of them will approach you from behind at an incredibly close distance, braking only at the last second. Anyone who has driven in hilly country, especially, knows what I'm talking about. Blasting their air horns, tailgating, and other forms of displaying their disdain for you who are in their way are common. But regardless of hilly terrain, flat lonely sections of highway, or city traffic, some truckers continually intimidate other drivers into getting out of the way.

However, despite the numbers of aggressive, dangerous truck drivers out there, we need to keep all things in context. *There are many thousands of excellent, safe truckers out there who deserve our admiration.* Again, I say, without the trucking industry and the products they deliver, the quality of our daily lives would be dramatically reduced. There are a lot of good guys out there, too, and it's important to remember that. They also have as much right (but not more) to be on the roads as the rest of us do.

Now, let's look deeper into the life of the truck driver. It might help us to better understand their predicament.

"When are You Coming Home Dad?"

Unlike many Americans who go home every night, most truckers must be away from home for many days, and sometimes weeks at a time. Birthdays, school events, anniversaries, holidays, and a host of other important occasions that most of us take for granted are often missed by the trucker. While we are feasting on a Thanksgiving turkey or helping a child learn to ride his or her first bike (both turkey and bike delivered by a trucker), the trucker is out there on some lonely road fighting the elements, bad drivers, city congestion, and his or her emotions. During holidays, as hundreds of us drive by these big rigs, our cars loaded down with gifts, the trucker can only look down and ache to be home with family.

At school, when other kids bring their moms and dads to Parent's Day, the trucker's kid is usually alone. If they're lucky, their mom or another relative can be there, but not always.

The trucking life is hard on families. It is a lonely, tedious existence where the truck driver is forced to be constantly on the move to make ends meet. Not unlike separations experienced by Navy and other military personnel, the emotional and physical toll on truckers and their families can be tremendous. And, like that of military personnel, the divorce rate among trucking families appears, at least when viewed from the outside, in my opinion, to be very high.

Impossible Deadlines - "Just-in-Time Deliveries"

Truckers, by federal law, must get eight hours sleep before driving 10 hours. They are required to fill out logbooks in which they record their activities, including rest periods, as evidence that they are abiding by the law. According to some experts, many drivers also have to spend as much as 20 hours per week just completing paperwork. When you add it all up, the demands on today's truckers are extreme.

During the same time that truckers have been forced to satisfy ever-increasing regulations, the trucking industry has become very competitive, and firms now compete with each other fiercely for customers. If a shipper calls up and demands that a product "absolutely must" be delivered by a certain time, hundreds or thousands of miles away, the trucking firm must meet the shipper's needs or lose crucial business.

Over time, with each successive "emergency shipment," the shipper soon begins to expect immediate delivery on all shipments. Or stated in a different way, what was once considered an exceptionally fast delivery time soon becomes the expected norm. The trucking firm must overcome the obstacles facing it or go out of business very quickly.

To compound matters, it is a logical path of thinking that manufacturers quickly learn to count on very fast delivery of their products by the trucking firms they use. As a result, company materials planners begin tightening delivery times to each other to accomplish the "just-in-time deliveries" we hear so much about, such as in the car manufacturing industry. By receiving parts and supplies just in time, these manufacturers need far less storage capacity and save on inventory taxes. This may be great for the manufacturers, but obviously, additional pressure is placed on the shoulders of truckers. If they don't make it to the factory on time, an entire production line can be shut down.

Factors such as the time of year (winter vs. summer) may be a part of the materials scheduling process, or they may not, depending on the skill and forethought of the materials schedulers. So, in essence, manufacturing plants may expect the same delivery times in weather sensitive northern areas in the winter time as they do in summer, with little thought about slower, more hazardous weather conditions or added driver fatigue.

After talking with a number of trucking firm experts, I've arrived at the conclusion that manufacturers simply do not care. They view these obstacles as simply the trucking firm's problem, not theirs. If they want the business, then they will just have to find a way to cope. If the trucking firm argues that they can't reasonably guarantee the delivery on time, the manufacturer simply gets on the phone and finds one of the many other trucking firms to serve their needs.

A Question of Liability

According to the trucking sources I talked with, many manufactures who once owned their own large trucking fleets are now using independent truckers or trucking firms to haul their goods. Where they once had to worry about truck maintenance, hiring drivers, and all the other issues that accompany the ownership of a viable fleet of trucks, they opt instead to let others haul their goods. They also don't have to worry about laying off drivers during slow periods.

However, as told to me by trucking insiders, there is another reason: liability. Simply put, in today's current legal quagmire of huge damage awards being given to accident victims, manufacturers are finding it more legally attractive to hire someone else to do the hauling for them.

It is common legal knowledge that when a lawsuit is filed, the entity with the deepest pockets, be it a person or corporation, is usually the one who ends up paying the largest share of the damage award. Therefore, these corporations have learned to avoid the problem by using third party shippers.

To many of these manufacturers, the independent drivers and small shipping companies are attractive. Not only is the trucking firm or independent driver forced to sign a complete waiver of liability (called indemnification) for the products being shipped, relieving the manufacturer of all liability, but the small trucking firm or independent driver is responsible for any damage to the goods being shipped as well.

For the goods manufacturers, all liability ends the moment the truck is loaded and leaves the manufacturer's property. For the trucking firm or independent, the scramble is on to get truck and driver to the manufacturer *now* to please the customer.

The truck driver often knows ahead of time that there is no way he or she can make the delivery schedule without breaking the federal government's work/sleep rules. Yet, if you don't work, you don't pay the bills. The trucker simply concedes his fate, accepts the load, and hits the road.

Over time, breaking the work/sleep rules becomes the normal expectation. The manufacturers press ever harder for shorter delivery times. Trucking firms continue to work at shaving a few hours here and there to please their customers. Over and over this scenario is repeated, wearing down the drivers, who are caught squarely in the middle.

A Severe Shortage of Drivers

Obviously, the truck driver is the one who loses in this game of raising the "fastest-delivery-time-ever bar" ever higher. They become very fatigued and frustrated. Recent nationwide studies show that many truck drivers admit to have fallen asleep at the wheel.

According to published reports and statistics generated by trucking related insurers, scores of truckers have become disenchanted and have left the trucking industry. They are seeking other forms of work.

One of the biggest concerns is that the *professional truck drivers*, the ones with the most experience, are leaving the industry in record numbers. To make matters worse, there aren't enough young drivers entering the ranks to replace those who have left. *The present driver shortage has reached an amazing 500,000 drivers.*

This driver shortage has in turn caused additional pressures within the industry as truckers, already fatigued and stretched to the limit, are forced to work even longer and harder.

Welfare Recipients as Truck Drivers

One industry official I spoke with said that some officials in the state of California are considering emptying their welfare roles by putting thousands of welfare recipients in the cabs of semi-tractor-trailer rigs due to the severe shortage of truckers there.

This scenario, if played out, could put many hundreds of inexperienced, possibly unsafe truck drivers on our roads. If such a welfare reduction move was even discussed as a way to fill, say, the pilot seats of airliners, the outcry would fill the halls of Congress. Yet, since these are "just trucks," little attention will most likely be paid to the issue.

Don't misunderstand: I'm not against the idea of placing capable, well trained, cool headed welfare recipients, foreigners, or anyone else behind the wheel of an 80,000 pound load. If they can read road signs, have the right depth perception, have good reaction time to be able to handle an emergency, etc., then why not. But to stick marginal or incapable drivers behind the steering wheels of these giant rigs just to fill the ranks and reduce the welfare rolls is disconcerting to many industry insiders and to this author.

However, as one trucking insider told me: "Any 16-year-old can run down to the license office, pass a simple test, and start driving a car that afternoon. Although he's a legal driver, he certainly has little or no experience yet. Even though a trucker's license (CDL) is a little tougher to get, with a little study, almost anyone can get one. Any way you look at it, a new truck driver behind the wheel of up to

80,000 pounds of steel and rubber, is as inexperienced as almost any 16-year-old behind the wheel of the family sedan."

Lumping

In the Trifon Lee Athnos story, we briefly discussed lumping. Essentially, lumping refers to the practice of forcing drivers to unload their trucks once they arrive at the customer's location.

In many cases, the driver is told upon arriving at the receiver's unloading dock that there is no one to unload them or that it will be "hours" before their dock personnel can get to their truck to unload it. Many of these drivers have no medical insurance. Yet, they are sometimes forced to unload an entire semi-trailer load by themselves, manually, sometimes injuring themselves.

At many docks, "lumpers" are hired by the drivers to help them unload their trucks. Lumpers are men who hang around loading docks and offer to unload the truck for the hapless driver for a cash fee. Truckers are often told that they have a very short time to unload their trucks at the dock before they must move their rig to allow other trucks to unload. With a time restriction as short as 20 minutes, the trucker often has no choice but to pay the lumpers what they demand to help unload his truck. Since the transaction is almost always in cash, the trucker is rarely reimbursed for his expense.

Do the shippers and receivers know about this practice? You bet they do. But again, this is cold, hard business, and they save a great deal of money by not having to hire dock personnel. These companies also know that time is money to the trucker, and that he needs to get back out onto the road and head for his next pickup.

A Need for Compassion

All drivers that share our roads have their own troubles. After all, we all have schedules to meet, bills to pay, problems at home and on the job, high taxes, etc. All of us are feeling the pressures of daily life in the late 90's and now, Y2K. It isn't easy making a living today.

However, I hope this chapter has helped the average driver to better understand the world of the trucker, who is forced to follow federal paperwork rules that in the words of one expert, "Would overwhelm many high paid corporate executives." Truckers must please their employers and customers by delivering goods over thousands of miles with little or no sleep, despite what the federal regulations say. If they don't deliver, they don't eat. They must pay lumpers to unload their trucks, often out of their own pockets. They must endure hours of driving through blizzards, violent storms, congested cities, and other hardships.

There are bad truck drivers out there, no doubt. While writing this book, I met several on the roads myself. But let us not condemn them all. Not everyone who drives an expensive German sports car drives like they're at the race track, either, caring little for others on the road: only some. It's the same with truckers.

So, when that trucker needs to merge into your lane, why not give him a break? Maybe if the average driving public began changing the way we drive around these big rigs, many truckers might be more civil themselves. Likewise, if the truckers out there who like to scare the living Hell out of average motorists in small cars would back off a little, maybe that would help too?

Any way you look at it, it will take all of us to turn the anger on our roads into tolerance and make them safer for us all.

Chapter Seventeen

Curbing a Mile-High Menace

The Mile-High City of Denver, Colorado, has seen a huge influx of people over the last 15 years. What used to be rolling, barren hills around Denver just a few years ago, are now sprawling developments, shopping centers, schools, etc. To keep pace, the state has done it's best to build new roads, such as the I-470 loop, to handle the dramatic increase in traffic.

However, it will be a long time before the current road building program can catch up with the traffic onslaught, which is a predictable result of such a quick increase in motor vehicles using Colorado's highways.

Road Rage is Getting Worse: Fact or Fiction?

One of the things that I wanted to find out while writing this book was whether the aggression on our roadways is really getting worse or am I and others just imagining it? There is a big difference between an accurate, definable, and measurable increase in road rage and aggressive driving, and a *"feeling"* that it's getting worse out there. The Colorado State Patrol offered some answers to this question.

"We've had a 200% increase in vehicle traffic in the last five years or so," says Captain Steve Powell, Colorado State Police Director of Public Affairs.

"We've backed off a little on the speeding issue. Don't misunderstand; we still write plenty of speeding tickets. However, we work for the people of Colorado, and they want us to help with the flow of traffic, not impede it. If traffic is moving smoothly at 10 miles over the limit, we usually do not intervene. However, the driver doing 15 or 20 miles over the limit is going to get nailed," he continued.

"The drivers that we are really concentrating on, are those who are driving dangerously. This includes weaving in and out of traffic, tailgaters, passing on the shoulder, and other types of behavior that in our experience, causes most of the accidents out there," Captain Powell continued.

Traffic Duty is Hazardous Work

I asked Captain Powell about his view of traffic enforcement, in regard to the safety of officers. His response was typical of other officers I spoke with across the nation:

"I tell my patrolmen, especially the newer guys, that for every one person out there who will shoot you, there are a hundred that will run you over along the side of the highway and say: *'Honey, did you hear a thump?'*" said Captain Powell.

Public Awareness Campaigns

Captain Powell went on to describe Colorado State Police efforts to get drivers to behave on Colorado highways:

"We're using printed materials, TV spots, personal appearances before students and adult groups, and anything else we can to get through to drivers. Hal Needham, who directed the movie 'Smokey and the Bandit,' did a TV commercial for us, which went over well. We are currently shipping the commercial to other states that have requested it," he said.

"We have also signed up all eleven of Colorado's cellular phone companies in our Cell Phone Reporting Program. Under this program, drivers can dial two different numbers to report bad drivers to us. We can respond immediately to some of the worst offenders, but we can also monitor and track, or "pattern" bad drivers over a period of time. Eventually, we send them a letter stating when and where the calls came in, and caution them that we know how they are driving, etc. In the worst cases, we can then begin to watch for them on our roads."

"We are also installing sophisticated equipment which allows us to detect if someone is abusing the system. For example, if someone just wants to get even with a neighbor and continually reports the same driver, we will know after a while that they are trying to use us to get at an innocent driver. Although it's not a perfect system, it is a way that the public can help us in changing the attitudes of our worst driving offenders," said the Captain.

Smile, You're on Van-Did Camera

Despite all of the Colorado State Patrol's efforts toward driver behavior modification, there are still many drivers who, in the end, will only respect a fat traffic ticket. For these folks, the Patrol has a few neat surprises.

"One of our most successful programs, is our 'Stealth Van,' said Powell. "We mount a camera in the back of a van, put a couple officers behind the camera, and hit the streets. We have all kinds of people tailgate us, challenge us, pass on the shoulder around us, etc. These folks are very surprised when we pull them over. The van has been very effective, especially in educating drivers on tailgating. We also get very few people who want to challenge us in court. Video tape doesn't lie."

Unnecessary Deaths

When I asked Captain Powell about how many traffic accidents Colorado is currently experiencing, his answer was again typical of most officers: "Too many. We lost 11 lives just last weekend. If we were losing that many citizens to murder every week, there would be a tremendous outcry. But because it's just a "traffic accident," most people just say to themselves "what a shame" and accept it. "Even most of our high schools no longer offer drivers education classes. We stop people 60 years old who don't even know about the *two-second rule*. Most say they have never heard of it," said the Captain.

"There is an amazing amount of ignorance out there on the roads. Many people today just do not realize what they are doing wrong. It is our job to enforce the law, but we could sure use some help on the education side. Fortunately, we are getting some help. Unfortunately, though, at times we are pressured by political forces to concentrate our efforts on other traffic issues, such as 'multi-occupant lanes'. I'm not saying that these issues aren't important. Saving fuel and thus helping to protect the environment, certainly is an important topic. However, not when it comes to diverting resources away from the immediacy of saving lives," Powell continued.

"When we are forced to give in to *political* issues, as opposed to life-saving *practical* issues, it places traffic officers in a difficult position. Unfortunately, that's part of the job."

Well said, Captain Powell.........

Increase in Aggressive Driving is Measurable

The Colorado State Patrol provided me with some statistics which clearly show the dramatic increase in non-speeding types of accidents, versus crashes caused by excessive speeds. The charts below illustrate that, overall, accidents in Colorado during the first quarter of 1998 are down from the first quarter of 1997. However, in Colorado, there has been a dramatic swing in the causes of accidents.

Accidents caused by speeding are down, as compared to the various types of aggressive maneuvers, as the primary cause of roadway accidents. Of these, the most dramatic increase in citations issued by the Colorado State Patrol is in the area of "tailgating" (following too close).

The patrol issued many more citations for following too close in the first quarter of 1998 than during the same period in 1997. Accidents caused by lane violations, failure to yield the right of way, improper passing, and disregarding stop signs, were also up.

These statistics are a dramatic example of where the patrol sees the most danger to motorists and illustrates how they are attacking the problem. They also illustrate that although drunk driving and speeding still contribute to a significant number of accidents, lane violations, tailgating, failure to yield, improper passing, and running stop signs account for three times the number of auto crashes that drunk drivers cause.

In a nutshell, aggressive driving and road rage are measurably on the rise, and this mean behavior is causing accidents and needless deaths.

In the chart below, you will see that the number of speeding tickets being written by the Colorado State Patrol has declined, though it is still significant. At the same time, tickets for aggressive driving have increased. Lane violations and following too close, two classic road rage behaviors and major causes of highway aggression, are measurably on the rise.

Curbing the Mile-High Menace

	Jan-Mar 1997		Jan - Mar 1998	
	Crashes	Citations	Crashes	Citations
Lane Violations	528	1,261	558	1,269
Following Too Close	390	*929	418	*1,375
Failing to Yield	351	467	386	499
Improper Passing	91	551	106	669
Wrong Side of Road	112	140	71	106
Disregarding Stop Sign	86	721	50	770
DUI	523	2,087	515	2,050
Total of Non-Speed	2,081	6,156	2,104	6,738
Exceeding Safe Speed	2,325	1,825	1,674	1,447
Exceeding Lawful Speed	274	16,431	214	12,635
Grand Total	4,680	24,412	3,992	20,820

	Percent of Change	
	Crashes	Citations
Lane Violations	+5.7%	+0.6%
Following Too Close	+7.2%	+48.0%
Failure to Yield	+10.0%	+6.9%
Improper Passing	+16.5%	+21.4%
Wrong Side of Road	-36.6%	-24.3%
Disregarding Stop Sign	-41.9%	+6.8%
DUI	-1.5%	-1.8%
Total of Non-Speed	+1.1%	+9.5%
Exceeding Safe Speed	-28.0%	-20.7%
Exceeding Lawful Speed	-21.9%	-23.1%
Grand Total	-14.7%	-14.7%

	Crashes		
	1997	1998	Change
Lane Violations	528	558	5.7%
Following Too Closely	390	418	7.2%

Although we've used Colorado as an example, law enforcement officials all over the United States are seeing increases in roadway aggression. Officials at local, state, and federal levels are carefully monitoring road rage and aggressive driving, and most are taking steps to curb this dangerous trend.

Demographics

One of the issues I set out to explore was the relationship between increases in population and road rage and aggressive driving. Denver has for a number of years, now, been singled out as a metropolitan area with an exploding population.

However, when I contacted the U.S. Census Bureau in Denver and discussed the city's population growth with them, I was shocked. They informed me that the Denver metropolitan area is nowhere near the top when it comes to population growth among U.S. cities: it's not even in the top 10 %.

From 1990 through 1996, the Denver metropolitan area grew by 15%. This is significant in that the total U.S. population grew by less than 1% during the same period. This 15% increase equates to a population growth of 980,140 people to 1,277,401, or an increase of about 297,000 people. However, the Denver area only ranks as number 33 on the list of the fastest growing U.S. metropolitan areas.

Colorado State Patrol
Covered Crashes
Cased by Aggressive Driving
Behavior

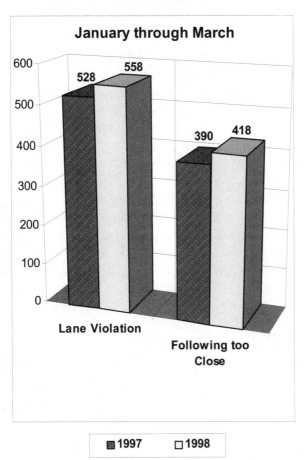

Source: Colorado State Highway Patrol

What this means is that even with the large increase in the population of the state of Colorado and their efforts to improve their road systems to accommodate the increase, there are 32 other major population centers that are growing even faster. One can assume, then, with some degree of assurance, that the measurable increase in aggressive driving that Colorado has experienced may be even worse elsewhere in the U.S.

Los Angeles, for example, seems to be where road rage first showed its ugly head, followed by New York, Chicago, and other major cities. Long known for its massive, traffic snarled freeways, California began to see shootings, fist fights, stabbings, vehicular assaults, and other aberrant behavior a long time ago. As with most trends in the U.S., they seem to start on the West Coast and migrate eastward.

But are road rage, aggressive driving, and other forms of bad roadway behavior limited to our large towns and cities? Not at all. As this book illustrates, road rage and aggressive driving are happening everywhere. From small towns in Oklahoma, to the corn fields of Iowa, to the small Amish communities of the Eastern Midwest, to small, rural communities everywhere, people are being terrorized and in some cases, attacked and killed on our roads.

But as illustrated in the case of Colorado, the drivers in the metropolitan areas of the U.S. are leading the way toward meaner, more hazardous roads in our country.

Chapter Eighteen

The UK and other Countries also Fight Road Rage

Cornhill Insurance is the largest auto insurer in Great Britain. Cornhill has been involved with the fight against road rage and aggressive driving for many years.

In one survey of British drivers, Cornhill sponsored researchers found that nearly 1 in 4 adults have committed an act of road rage. In addition, the survey showed that men are almost three times more likely to commit an aggressive driving act than women.[45]

Road Rage "Commuter Combat in America"

The market research company RGSB surveyed more than 1,000 people as part of Cornhill's campaign to emphasize to the public that road rage-type behavior is completely unacceptable to insurers, and convictions resulting from aggressive driving will result in increased premiums and possibly cancellation of coverage.

Cornhill has distributed a "Keep Calm Code" leaflet, which is aimed at helping victims deal more effectively with aggression from other road users. The program has been well received by police and road safety officers, with over 500,000 copies circulated annually.

Cornhill, which looked at the issue of road rage from the victim's viewpoint, was interested in profiling the likely perpetrators of aggression. The research found:

- **1 in 5 acts of road rage involve intimidatory driving.**
- **61% are acts of verbal abuse with 50% involving aggressive hand gestures.**
- **30% of aggression is perpetrated by people in the 25-34 age group. However, road rage is not confined to any age or social class.**

According to Denis Loretto, Cornhill's Director and General Manager, "The message that road rage is unacceptable does not appear to be getting across." He added: "The message should be a multi-agency approach to this problem, involving government, police, and insurers. We have already reported that 84% of people believe a person's character changes for the worse when they get behind the wheel. People are being killed or injured as a result."

Chapter Nineteen

A Few Personal Notes on Road Rage

A Saturday from Hell

It's 10:05 in the morning, and Lori is headed for the door. Since it's Saturday, Lori and I had gotten up a little later than usual, but not by much. The alarm goes off at 4:00 am during the week, which is a tad earlier than most folks, for sure. If this author is to beat the traffic jams, he's got to get up and be gone before most folks even roll out of bed. But even on weekends, we still get up pretty early. We like to spend time together, and since she works a lot of weekends, we have to grab whatever moments we can.

She gives me a kiss goodbye and I tell her to drive safely. In a flash, I'm back at the computer toiling away on the book you're reading now.

It's 10:35 and the portable phone rings. Before I can even say hello, Lori, recognizing my voice and crying hysterically, begins to half scream into the receiver. I back the phone away from my ear, now hurting, and try my best to make out what she is trying tell me. After she calms down, she's finally able to convey to me what had happened.

"I came up over the hill on 55 near Barnhardt, and a semi was stopped right in front of me. I locked up my brakes, but I had this damn semi right on my tail and he couldn't stop," she said (sobbing hard now). "There were cars to my left...we were on the bridge, too. I had nowhere to go but into the right lane, which was actually the exit ramp. I got over, and the semi behind me almost ran into the one in front of me. He locked up and stopped just inches from the other semi. If there had been a car on my right, I wouldn't have been able to get over and I would be dead now!" she continued. "That idiot was right on my butt for miles and I couldn't shake him. He could have killed me!"

After we talked for a while and I got her calmed down, and made sure she was OK, she asked me to call her boss and tell her that she was going to be late. Her makeup was all over her face from crying, and it would take a while for her to fix herself up and regain her composure. I hung up, called her boss, and let her know what had happened.

I turned and looked at the clock on the wall. "I could have lost her today," I said to myself. "The kids could have lost their mother today...April 29, 1998. Write this time and date down for the book. Remember what happened this day."

A Little Side Errand

It's 11:15 now, and Scotty, 8, our youngest boy, is with me as I head down the driveway to work. I need to put in a few hours at the office to catch up. Scotty can play with his trucks on my office floor.

As we approach the Highway 270 and Highway 40 interchange, I decide to go on ahead up to the lawn tractor dealer and pick up a new gas cap for the riding mower. It's only a few miles out of the way and won't take long.

I glance in the mirror, and notice a lady in a small car following too closely. Ahead of me (at a safe following distance I should add) is a shiny Jaguar XJ6 Sedan. "Nice car," I say to myself. An older woman, obviously of substantial means, is behind the wheel.

Moments later I notice two more Jaguar XJ6's ahead pulled over to the outside shoulder. At almost the same instant, the lady in the Jag ahead of me locks 'em up. She obviously has recognized the two other ladies standing next to their Jaguars. Obviously, one of them is having some sort of mechanical difficulty.

I stand on my brakes with all I've got to avoid hitting her. No time to worry about the lady in the little car behind me.....she's on her own. I hope she doesn't hit me, but I'm too busy trying to avoid the Jaguar, now at a complete stop, dead in the slow lane ahead. No signal, no warning, no attempt to pull off the road. She had just decided to lock up her brakes and stop.

I'm sliding now, half sideways. I come to a stop just inches from her rear bumper. Briefcase, books, spilled sodas, all co-mingled on the floorboard. I glance up and see the lady in the little car behind me fishtailing wildly as she tries to avoid my F-150's rear end. She just makes it.

The Jaguar lady, either by hearing my squealing tires or seeing the truck grill filling up her rearview mirror, has now realized her error and floors her car as she pulls off onto the shoulder. Once there, she slams on the brakes again, sending gravel flying.

Get Out of the Road!

Badly shaken, I somehow still have enough of my wits to find the gas pedal and get going again before the lady behind me and I get hit by someone else. Simultaneously, I reach over and put my hand on Scotty (always in his seat belt from habit and parental nagging) and check to make sure he's OK. As I glance at him, he has a look of true shock on his face. He doesn't speak for quite some time. *This one was really close.*

Folks, this author does a LOT of driving, and I've learned to handle myself pretty well in most situations. But I must tell you that this event happened so fast and was so stupid (her acquaintances had not been in an accident; there was no emergency) that it took everything in me to not stop and let her know how I felt. She had endangered my life and that of my son, not to mention the drivers behind me.

Somehow, I forced myself to remember how we can all make mistakes. I didn't scream, I didn't gesture, I didn't pull over and give her a piece of my mind. I continued on down the road and pulled over. Scotty and I grabbed whatever we could, especially the spilling cokes, and picked up the floorboard.

I sat there quietly for a few minutes. I looked at my watch and rubbed Scotty's bushy head. My hands were shaking as we talked about what had just happened. "Stupid lady", the eight year-old blurts out. "If I was a cop, I'd give her a heck of a ticket."

Just hearing his little voice and the ever honest comments he, like all kids, makes, reassured me that he was OK. I thought maybe, no, I'm sure, that having him with me shook me up a lot more than I would have been. I said a little prayer of thanks. For good brakes. *For seat belts used.*

I look back at my watch: 12:15. "This is a Saturday from Hell," I mutter to myself. "Gosh Dad, Mom almost got killed this morning and us too!" he reasons.

"Yeah Buddy, that was close. Too close," I respond.

"Man, Dad, that old lady is going to get someone killed," he says again, as we pull back onto the road and continue on to the lawn mower parts store.

He talks for 30 minutes about bad drivers as we get the part and complete the trip to work. Once there, I have a hard time concentrating for quite some time. This was a quiet, light traffic day. A Saturday, and yet, a few idiots on the road could have wiped out a mother, a father, and the youngest of six children. And in separate accidents.

This driving is dangerous business!

Three Weeks Later: Four Die on Hwy 44

It's May 18, just three weeks after Lori was nearly killed on the road and Scotty and I had our close call. The Monday morning radio describes a horrific accident on Highway 44, just a short drive from where Lori was almost sandwiched between the two semi's.

The radio describes two vehicles, one a sport utility vehicle, the other a van, which were smashed between two semi-trucks. A man and his little two-year-old son in the SUV are dead. So is the couple in the van. The truck drivers are reported to be unhurt.

Apparently, an accident ahead had stopped traffic. It seemed that the SUV hit the back of the first truck, then the van struck the back of the SUV. That was bad enough, but when the huge semi behind them couldn't stop, their death was certain.

"That could have been Lori," I say to myself. "My God, when are people going to stop following so close? Don't they know we're killing each other out here? Doesn't anyone give a damn!?"

A Final Word
Get Some Help

If you are one who is prone to road rage, seek help. Don't wait until you kill someone's princess or prince in a fit of rage. If you know someone who is violent behind the wheel, try to reach them, please. It is going to take all of us to stop this epidemic of roadway violence.

If you think you are a good driver, think hard about it. Are you really? All the time? When this author began to research material for this book, he thought he was a good driver, too. He wasn't as good, or at least as "kind" to others on the road as he should have been. He's better now. But first, he had to admit that he could drive better, be more patient, more tolerant and gentle on the road. If I can admit it, maybe you can, too.

Protecting Yourself

People are espousing so many methods of controlling road rage, both for self-protection and self-control, that it's hard to know where to begin. One government official I talked to, said she put stickies all over her dash with calming notes. What about keeping our eyes on the road?

There are several books available that cover the subject in great detail. Here are a few ideas you might consider:

Self Control and Confrontations:

Don't take it personally.
Listen to calming tapes.
Don't make eye contact with an offender.
Don't hit your brakes - get out of the way.
Report dangerous drivers.
Don't pull over. And don't get out of your vehicle.
Go to a police station if possible, if being followed.
Drive with the flow of traffic.
Don't drive slow in the fast lane.
Don't take on a semi. You'll lose!
Use your turn signals.
Do not give hand gestures. You may be killed.
Adjust your driving times, if possible.
Telecommute, if possible.

Remember, we teach others how to treat us. We can all make a difference. Let it start with you!

The Middle Third

One Last Comment:

I recently heard another author make an interesting analogy in regard to Americans and how we act nowadays. He said: "I believe, that 20 years ago, one- third of us were saints, one-third were sinners, and the one-third of us in the middle usually tried to do the right thing," he said. "Today, I believe one-third of us are still saints, one-third of us are still sinners, but the one-third of us in the middle now do whatever will gain us the most." I believe that this author is right on target. Our roads are meaner today, quite possibly because we have lost those of us in the middle third to a hard-driving desire to gain that competitive edge. To one-up the other guy.

Only by driving kindly, can we ever hope to change others. We learn from each other, copy each other, emulate each other's actions. Now that you have read this book, won't you help by doing your part?

Drive carefully, please. The next fatality could be you.

Highway Safety Web Sites and Addresses

AAA - Foundation for Traffic Safety
1440 New York Avenue, N.W.
Washington, D.C. 20005
202/638-5944
http://www.aaafts.org/

MADD - Mothers Against Drunk Driving
http://www.busprod.com/walker/madd/pg1.htm

SADD - Students Against Destructive Decisions
http://www.geocities.com/missourisadd/

NHTSA - National Highway Transportation
Safety Administration
 www.nhtsa.dot.gov

Partnership for Safe Driving
www.roadrights.com

Driver/Education Newsletter
http://www.pde.drivers.com/driv-ed.html

Defensive Driving:

Clarity Multimedia® CD-ROM Course
1-888-421-9954

Help for the Aggressive Driver:

"When Anger Hurts" (for Kids) by Matthew McKay, Peter D. Rogers, and Judith McKay (New Harbinger Publications; $15.95)

"Anger at Work: Learning the Art of Anger Management on the Job" by Hendrie Weisinger (Morrow, William and Co. $12.00)

"Anger Kills: Seventeen Strategies for Controlling the Hostility That Can Harm Your Health" by Redford and Virginia Williams (Harper Collins $13.00)

"Anger Disorders: Definition, Diagnosis and Treatment," Howard Kassinove (Taylor and Francis, Inc. $29.95)

"Controlling Anger Before it Controls You" free from the American Psychological Association. Write to: Office of Public Affairs, 750 First St. NW. Washington, D.C., 20002 or at: www.helping.apa.org/daily/anger.html

Additional Road Rage Reading

Road Rage to Road Wise, John A. Larson
ISBN 0312890583, Forge

The 10-Step Compassion Program for Overcoming Road Rage (Pocket Guide) Arnold Nerenberg

Dr. Leon James (Dr. Driving)
http://www.aloha.net/

The Peaceful Driver, Allen Liles
ISBN 0871598574 Unity House

John Deere Transportation Insurance
Http://www.deere.com

Index

Abernathy, Ronald 69-76
Alfieri, Tracie 43
Algoa Correctional Facility, 32
Andrews, Rene 43
Althorp Mansion, 34
Archer, Mike, DA   31
Athnos, Trifon Lee 69- 86
Beyers, Bryan 107
Blatt, Jessie 124
Boshea, Robert 53
Brake Slamming, 39 - 44
Brueggemann, Charles, Lt. 134
Butler, Daniel Wesley 59
Carter, Ken 133,134
Cline, David 46
Costello, Catherine 41
Cornhill 206
Curt, 26
Culver, Bill DA 68
Curran, Shawn Neal 86
Davis, Michael 69 - 76
Denny, Daniel 42
Devanny, John 23, 30 - 33
Estok, George 182
Fifteen Minutes (poem), 37
Frank, Tiffany 44
Ganapathy, Raj 160 - 162
Glerum, William 49
Graham, Donald 95
Hardick, Richard 56
Hixon, David 98
Hogg, Buffy Marie 51
Hywari, Jennifer Lynn 25 - 37
Just-in-Time Deliveries 186
Katie, 21
Kelsey, Kenny 48
KMOX, 22
Koenigs, Denise 48
Lewis, Troy Sgt. 128 - 143
Lierman, Jennettie & Mike 27 - 36
Loretto, Denis 206
Loring, Ben DA 68
Lumping, 191
Macklin, Jon David 46
MacPhee, Laura 63
MacPhee, Patrick 64
Marston, Brett 57

Martinez, Ricardo Dr. 119
Matton, Laurens 63
McAmis, John 53, 54
McCoy, Tony 76
McKnight, Jim 124
Mohr, Shaun 44
Morrison, Jamie 66
Naranjo, Pedro 58
NHTSA, 117 - 125
Partnership for Safe Driving, 34
Princess Diana, 33, 34
Powers, Richie 69 - 76
Powell, Steve Capt. 196 - 200
Protecting Yourself, 213
Pruett, Max Michael 59
Purnell, David, 53
Qualcom Messages, 78 - 85
Rage, 12
Rogers, Laura 87
Rubalcalvas, Marco 59
Salas, Luis 66
Saucedo, Abmielec 56
Scully, Timmy 58
Sembach Sr., David 59
Shootings, 61 - 66
Stabbings, 51 - 53,56
Stokes, Paul Sgt. 128 - 143
Strackta, Mark 90, 148 - 154
The Middle Third, 214
Trip, 172 - 175
Tyson, Mike 56
Van Lear, Jerald 48
Vehicle Ramming, 45, 47
Walters, Joseph Burl 62
Weckesser, Mark 48
Welch Jr., Martell 60
Wiggins, Kraal 44
Wilkins, William M. 173 -175
Word, Deletha 60

Footnotes

[1] Akron Beacon Journal, July 15, 1999
(Police Seek Suspect in Road Rage Beating) Joe Kiefer
[2] St. Louis Post Dispatch, April 10, 1998
("Road Rage Case Ends in Conviction, Tears in
Courtroom") William C. Lhotka
[3] Star Tribune, Minneapolis, Minn., July 19, 1997
("Road rage Cited as Highway Deaths Increase") Jaurie
Blake
[4] The Arizona Republic, September 10, 1999
("Veteran Firefighter is Charged in Loop 101 Road Rage
Accident") Judi Villa
[5] The Cincinnati Post, January 1, 1999
("Court Upholds Fetus Law") Sharon Moloney
[6] The Cincinnati Post, September 13, 1999
("Driver Charged in Assault") Staff Report
[7] The Advocate, Baton Rouge, LA May 10, 1999
("Deadly Crash Kills 23")
[8] The San Diego Union-Tribune, October 16, 1997
("Driver Ed Teacher Punches Motorist")
[9] Albuquerque Journal, October 12, 1999
("Passenger Hurt in I-40 Wreck") Jeff Jones
[10] The Akron Beacon Journal, August 15, 1999
(Akron Driver Accused of Ramming Vehicle)
[11] The Detroit News, March 22, 1999
(Road Rage Outcry on the Rise) B.G. Gregg
[12] Wisconsin State Journal, August 25, 1999
(Charges filed in Road Rage Case)
[13] The San Diego Union-Tribune, September 4, 1997
(Driver Sentenced in Road Rage Case)
[14] States News Service, August 15, 1997
(Charges Filed in Stabbing Incident)
[15] The Detroit News, May 15, 1997
(Driver Filled with Road Rage Stabs Motorist in
Lansing) Kenneth Cole
[16] Associated Press, February 4, 1998
("Driver Beaten Unconscious after Running Red Light
and Causing Crash")
[17] Journal Sentinel Inc. June 10, 1997
("Freeway Spat Escalates Between Professor, Federal
Agent")

[18] The Baltimore Sun, February 6, 1999
(Tyson Returns to Jail in Road rage Ruling) Candus Thomson

[19] Capitol Times, Madison, Wisconsin, Sept. 27, 1999
(Cops Say Cab Driver Kicked Pregnant Woman over Fare)
[20] Capitol Times, Madison, Wisconsin, Sept. 27, 1999
(Thursday Evening Road Rage Led to Mass Fight) Police report
[21] The San Diego Tribune, June 10, 1998
(Road Rage Escalates into Face Slashing) Joe Hughes
[22] Times Union, Jacksonville, Florida July 21, 1997
("On the Road to Rage: Aggressive Driving Rates Rising")
Sean Gardiner
[23] The San Diego Tribune, May 27, 1998
(Teen is Killed in Road Attack)
[24] The San Diego Tribune, June 29, 1996
(Experts Offer Tips on How to Tame Behind the Wheel Beast) Shankar Vedantam
[25] Times Union, Jacksonville, Florida July 21, 1997
("On the Road to Rage: Aggressive Driving Rates Rising")
Sean Gardiner
[26] St. Paul Pioneer Press, August 3, 1997
("Aggressive Driving Erupting into Road Rage") Sara Goo
[27] APB 911 News, April 19, 1999
("Father Charged with Road Rage Killing of Son") Pete Bush
[28] Phone Interview, Deputy DA Laura Rogers, 1998
[29] Phone Interview, Sergeant Strackhta, 1998
[30] The Denver Post, November 26, 1999
(Road Rage Blamed for Head-On Wreck) Mike Soraghan
[31] Police Report No. 2292, Freedom of Information Act, Illinois State Police, 6/10/98.
[32] Wisconsin State Journal, September 24, 1999
(Road Rage Lands Merrimac Man in Jail) Kathleen Ostrander
[33] Yahoo, Collection of Road Rage Stories
[34] Albuquerque Tribune Web Page, July 12, 1997
("Bike Wheels Keep on Turnin") J. Gutierrez Kruege

Footnotes

[35] LCC Web Page, London, England, November 11, 1997
(*"Woman Jailed for Running Down Cyclist"*)
[36] Albuquerque Tribune Web Page, July 12, 1997
(*"Bike Wheels Keep on Turnin'"*) J. Gutierrez Kruege
[37] Interview: Bryan Byers, Ball University, 1998
[38] Public Employee, January/February, 1998
(*"It's Scary Out There!"*)
[39] Public Employee, January/February, 1998
(*"It's Scary Out There!"*)
[40] NHTSA News Release: Web Page
[41] Indianapolis Star, April 20, 1999
(*"Bill to Protect Police on Roadside is Signed"*) Kristin
Glazner
[42] TRIP Report Web Page
[43] Sharing the Road, John Deere Insurance/Interview
[44] Sharing the Road, John Deere Insurance/Interview
[45] Cornhill Report

To Order Additional Copies of this book:

Send $13.95 + $3.00 S&H each to:
Silvertip Books
P.O. Box 365
Herculaneum, MO 63048

(Missouri Residents add $1.04 state tax per book)

Toll Free Number
(Credit Card Orders Only):   1-877-937-6707

Include shipping address with your order

Distributors, Wholesalers, and Retail Inquiries,
Quantity Orders:

1-(636)-937-5952 or toll free: 1-(877)-937-6707

Fax: (636) 937-6707